PUPPY TRAINING FOR BEGINNERS

THE COMPLETE GUIDE TO RAISING YOUR PUPPY
AND BECOMING HIS BEST FRIEND

Colin Farley

© **Copyright 2020 by Colin Farley**

All rights reserved.

This document is geared towards providing exact and reliable information with regards to the topic and issue covered. The publication is sold with the idea that the publisher is not required to render accounting, officially permitted, or otherwise, qualified services. If advice is necessary, legal or professional, a practiced individual in the profession should be ordered.

From a Declaration of Principles which was accepted and approved equally by a Committee of the American Bar Association and a Committee of Publishers and Associations.

In no way is it legal to reproduce, duplicate, or transmit any part of this document in either electronic means or in printed format. Recording of this publication is strictly prohibited and any storage of this document is not allowed unless with written permission from the publisher. All rights reserved.

The information provided herein is stated to be truthful and consistent, in that any liability, in terms of inattention or otherwise, by any usage or abuse of any policies, processes, or directions contained within is the solitary and utter responsibility of the recipient reader. Under no circumstances will any legal responsibility or blame be held against the publisher for any reparation, damages, or monetary loss due to the information herein, either directly or indirectly.

Respective authors own all copyrights not held by the publisher.

The information herein is offered for informational purposes solely, and is universal as so. The presentation of the information is without contract or any type of guarantee assurance.

The trademarks that are used are without any consent, and the publication of the trademark is without permission or backing by the trademark owner. All trademarks and brands within this book are for clarifying purposes only and are owned by the owners themselves, not affiliated with this document.

TABLE OF CONTENTS

PART I 1

CHAPTER ONE 2

Why Train a Dog? 2
    Establishing Objectives 4
    Dogs are Friends of a Lifetime. 4
    Make Time to Practice 5

CHAPTER TWO 7

Understanding How Dogs Know 7
    Understanding Instincts 7
    Dogs Have Feelings and Emotions 8
    Breeds Make a Difference 10
    Understanding Puppy Development 14
    A Long Way from Wolves 17
    Early Training and Socialization Benefits 19

CHAPTER THREE 21

Interacting with Your Dog 21
    First, Get the Behavior, Then Add the Signal 22

Using Appropriate Cues to Achieve the Best Results --- 23

THE BODY TELLS A TALE --- 26

Ears --- 26

Eyes --- 27

Mouth --- 27

Tail --- 28

Overall Body Posture --- 29

Signs of Stress --- 30

Dog's Senses --- 34

The All-Knowing Nose --- 34

Can Dogs Hear? --- 37

Taste and Feel --- 38

CHAPTER FOUR --- 40

Emphasize The Positive! --- **40**

Understanding the Scientific Principles of Training --- 42

Classical Conditioning --- 43

Operant Conditioning --- 45

Training Behaviors Step-by-Step --- 48

Step 1: Get the Behavior --- 48

Shaping --- 50

Capturing --- 52

Modeling --- 53

Step 2: Note the Behavior and Reward It --- 53

Step 3: Add a Cue --- 57

Step 4: Train to Fluency --- 58

Reward-Based Learning --- 61

Attention and Affection --- 63

Verbal Praise --- 64

Food Incentive -- 65

Toys -- 68

Play -- 69

Life Rewards -- 70

Introducing the Clicker -- 70

Introducing a Target --- 71

Introducing a Nose Target -- 72

Introducing a Paw Target --- 74

PART II --- 78

CHAPTER FIVE --- 79

Early Training --- 79

What You'll Need --- 81

Leash -- 81

Collar --- 82

Harness -- 83

Head Halter --- 84

Clicker --- 85

Crate -- 86

Toys --- 88

Good Exercise Makes a Healthy Dog -------------------------------- 92

Exercise and Weather --------- 95

The Secret to Good Puppy Training --------- 97

CHAPTER SIX --------- 100

House-Training --------- 100

Crate Training --------- 102

Crate Location --------- 104

Crate Accessories --------- 105

Introduction of the Crate --------- 106

Setting Schedules --------- 111

Training Your Puppy to Potty Outside --------- 113

Training Your Puppy to Excrete While Indoors --------- 118

Future Training --------- 122

Teaching Your Puppy to Ring a Bell --------- 124

Cleaning Up Messes --------- 126

CHAPTER SEVEN --------- 128

Basic Etiquette and Life Skills --------- 128

Safety Net: The Collar and Leash of Your Dog --------- 130

Bite Inhibition --------- 135

Nail Clipping --------- 141

Happy Vet Visits --------- 142

CONCLUSION --------- 145

PART I

THE BASICS OF DOG TRAINING

CHAPTER ONE

WHY TRAIN A DOG?

There is a commitment to having a dog as a member of the family. You need to make sure he has the right health care. You need to make sure to feed him healthy foods. You will need to help him understand how to work with people and, more importantly, how to work with your family as a good partner.

As much of a bond as most dogs have to humans, they are not born to learn how to live with us. Dogs are different animals than humans, so they come with their own breed-specific habits. Such actions can also stand in contrast to our human standards of acceptable behavior.

When you grow into adults, grown-ups taught you life skills. Some of these adults may have been better teachers than others, but you grew up learning how to act at home and out in public. What is appropriate in your community may have varied marginally from what was appropriate in your neighbor's community, but in general, you have mastered simple good-citizen skills. Now, you need to teach your dog the same skills.

Inherently, the dog doesn't know that he's not supposed to urinate on your couch or climb on you and knock you down. He doesn't have a manual to justify why he can't chew on your favorite shoes or shirt. He has no idea what the "indoor sound" is like. He also doesn't know that he can't just run up and get in the face of another dog or dig in your neighbor's precious rose garden. You need to tell him all these things, and you do!

Part of being a responsible pet owner is showing your dog proper family hygiene, and making sure it's not a public nuisance.

Through teaching your dog with reward-based, constructive approaches, you are serving these obligations.

Did you happen to notice that? Training is mutually beneficial.

A really well-trained dog is pleasant to work with and is also accepted in many places. If you're going to travel with your dog, even if it's just to a relative's house, he's going to need to have manners so he doesn't embarrass you or cause trouble. Training your dog helps build your relationship as you learn to understand each other better. And the sweet compliments you get on the actions of your dog are a plus!

Establishing Objectives

There's nothing wrong in attempting to set expectations for your dog. You may have aspirations of training the champion of agility or wanting to share your dog with others as a therapy dog. Study what you need to accomplish these goals and start training your dog to accomplish them. You're going to focus on getting there together.

Another duty you have is to appreciate your dog for what it is. Understand that not every dog is suitable to every activity. Each dog is a different breed. He will never compare to any of the former dogs you've ever had, and you'll never have another dog like him again.

Dogs are Friends of a Lifetime.

Your dog is unique in its own way, even if it never turns out to be a champion of agility or a dog for therapy. You will find that you need to change your expectations when you continue your training plan and learn more about the strengths and challenges of your dog. Although shifting your standards can be really disappointing at first, you're still going to have something fantastic in your favor— your puppy. No matter what you're doing, your dog is going to accept you, and that is really something to be cherished.

Make Time to Practice

There is no fixed time when training is best. What's working for you? What's working for your dog? Are you a morning person? Teach your dog when you get up first. Are you a night owl? In the evenings, train your puppy. Your training plan will be as flexible as you need it to be. The most important thing is to get going and keep it up every day.

Almost all of the people who attempt this are really busy. Most don't know how tough a dog, particularly a young puppy, is to train. If you're using constructive techniques, you don't need a lot of time to train your dog— only fifteen minutes is enough to do the trick, and not even fifteen minutes in a string.

Training sessions should be just a few minutes long, so it's easy to squeeze in fifteen minutes of the day, particularly because you can train during your daily routine.

For instance, every morning you have to take your dog out on a leash as part of your house-training program. At the same time you do this, you will train the Wait Cue. Wait Cue means that your dog needs to wait in place before you order him to do something else, so it's a very useful action to help keep your dog from running out the door. If you train Wait while you're going inside and outside for all of your dog's potty breaks, you're going to have a lot of repetitions in fast bursts all day long. Going to wait at the door, waiting for your go ahead, so he can go through can become a habit for your dog.

It is best to define house rules before you bring your dog home as it can be very difficult for your dog if you teach him a set of behaviors and then decide later that they are not suitable. What are the rules of your house? Would you like to have your dog on the furniture? Or in the bedroom at night? Is it all right if he sits on you? Is it all right if he kisses your face? What do you want him to get rid of? If you have other dogs in your house, how would you like him to communicate with them? For instance, if you have a senior dog and you bring a puppy home, what do you think is appropriate to your older dog?

Set some guidelines and teach your dog to follow them. Be compliant with that. Be sure your family and all other housemates are on the same page, otherwise it's going to be really difficult to train your puppy. He's not going to understand if you don't let him get on the bed, however, your roommate does while you're out of town.

CHAPTER TWO

UNDERSTANDING HOW DOGS KNOW

Dogs are a different species from what we are. Behavior that you find abnormal as a human is always, in canine terminology, natural. Envision getting up in the morning surrounded by people who are using a language that you don't understand and who have strange customs. You will learn a new vocabulary and what this culture considers acceptable and unacceptable, but someone will have to teach you in a language that you will comprehend. This is the job you get to do for your dog.

Understanding Instincts

Dogs spontaneously dig and leap and chase and bark and perform other typical behaviors of their species. Those are the natural activities of dogs.

When you take a lovely walk down the street and your dog sees a squirrel, it may automatically run after it. It doesn't mean that you have to accept behaviors that you don't like, but it helps you understand what behaviors are common for dogs.

Some breeds have been deliberately designed to do unique things. Many dogs have been fine-tuned to hunt for livestock, while others have been trained to follow the smell. Such habits are now embedded in these breeds, and it's normal for them to do so. The dog isn't being stubborn or aggressive when he's only reacting to his genes.

Dogs Have Feelings and Emotions

Anybody who has ever loved a dog will tell you that dogs have emotions and feelings, and a new study has confirmed that dog owners have been right from the get-go. Gregory Berns, Professor of Neuroeconomics at Emory University in Atlanta, Georgia, has completed work showing that dogs use the same brain regions as humans. Berns found parallels in the structure and function of the brain region called the caudate nucleus. In humans, the caudate nucleus reacts in anticipation of things we enjoy, such as love, food, and money. Among dogs, Berns' work showed that the caudate nucleus responds to hand signals signaling food and the smells of familiar humans.

Initial testing also showed that the caudate nucleus responded to the return of the owner of the dog after the owner had briefly stepped out of sight.

What the study has actually shown is that dogs have a degree of consciousness like a human being, which is no surprise to anyone who has ever loved a dog. How else do you feel, other than joy, when your dog greets you after your absence? If you've ever seen those heart-warming videos of servicemen and servicewomen coming back from deployment to greet their happy pets, how could there be any doubt? If you've ever lost one dog to a few, don't the others want to mourn?

Dogs are thinking, emotional creatures, whether or not science has kept up with what we think is real. It is vital when it comes to picking a training program. If the dogs can hear, do you want to harm them in order to teach them? Of course not. And you don't have to — there are constructive ways to teach your dog to do what you want him to do.

Breeds Make a Difference

Your dog's breed or breed combination can have an effect on its behavior. Humans have selectively bred dogs to perform various tasks over time, and eventually come up with specific breeds. There are hundreds of dog breeds on the planet. When you have a mixed-breed dog, you may have to guess who their parents are if you don't get a chance to meet them. Many times you can tell the breed from looking at the puppy's features, but you can also look at the behavior of your puppy.

If your purebred dog has characteristics of race that you don't like, who can you blame? You're the one who picked the dog for you. This doesn't mean that you have to bear with constant chasing or barking or hunting, so please don't get angry at your dog for doing what he was brought up to do.

The American Kennel Club (AKC) divides dog breeds with common characteristics into classes. Let's examine some of the features of these classes.

Herding Breeds

Herding breeds have been developed to transport livestock. Many breeds specialize in horses, some with goats, and others are used for multi-species. Some push livestock by barking at them, while others nibble at their feet. Essentially, herding breeds are particularly good at catching stuff and rounding them up. People sometimes complain that their herding dog is chasing their children or the family pet.

Herding breeds are generally very quick and strong, and they do very well in speed sports, such as agility. They are always active dogs, so they do their best when you give them healthy choices to channel that energy.

Sporting Breeds

Sporting breeds have been created to work with hunters. Some flush prey, some retrieve, and some point where the prey is hidden. Many of them specialize in working in the water, and some are better in the field. Some also perform several tasks.

Sporting-bred dogs typically have a lot of energy, particularly as puppies and adolescents. They work very well with people in general and are famous family dogs. Breeds in this group include Labrador Retriever, English Setter, Golden Retriever, Portuguese Water Dog, and Brittany.

Hound Breeds

Hounds were raised for hunting. Few (such as the Basset Hound) excel at following scent, and some (such as the Whippet) hunt by sight. Such breeds are long-lasting and have endurance. Some of them even bay. Breeds in this group include Greyhound, Bloodhound, Beagle, Irish Wolfhound, and Afghan Hound.

Terrier Breeds

Terriers have been trained to track and kill vermin. They're stubborn, they have a lot of strength, and they can be feisty. Many of them have wiry coats that require special treatment, called stripping, to keep up their look. You may note that your terrier likes to "strike" his toys by shaking them.

Toy Breeds

These little dogs have been developed to be companions. As a result, they are very knitted to their families, and they always follow them around. Their sheer size makes them perfect for living in an apartment, but don't dare to tell a Toy breed dog that he's tiny. He's not going to believe you! Breeds in this group are Papillon, Chihuahua, Maltese, Pomeranian, and Pug.

Working Dogs

Working dogs were trained to do tasks, such as protecting land, pulling sleds, and other duties. Since all the tasks are special, so are the individual dogs. Generally, these dogs are typically strong and loyal, and some are very tall.

Non-Sporting

The Non-Sporting category is a kind of catchall for a range of breeds, and the dogs in it are all over the globe in terms of size and behavioral characteristics. The Shiba Inu, for instance, is a small Japanese dog bred to hunt small wild game, boar, and bear. The Chow Chow is a variable-sized Chinese dog used for hunting, defending, pushing, and herding. Many breeds in this group include Schipperke, Bichon Frise, and Poodle.

Miscellaneous

The AKC also has a separate section. This classification is intended for purebred dogs who are "on deck" to be added to the rosters of a daily category. In order to progress to a regular class, breeds must have an active parent club and a 'significant and increasing breeding operation across a wide geographical region.' Such breeds may already be recognized in other countries; there are several breeds active in other countries that are not yet registered with

AKC, probably because they are not as common in the United States as they are in other countries.

Understanding Puppy Development

Puppies begin to learn right after birth, so it's crucial to understand what's going on in those vital first weeks of existence.

Puppies learn several lessons from their parents and their siblings. Mothers have to wash the puppies so that they can urinate and defecate, and then they also wipe the pups clean. That's how the puppies figure out how to stay healthy. If they don't have this contact with Mom because they were taken away from her too early, they can have difficulty learning home-training later; this is also a concern for puppies purchased from pet stores.

Puppies cultivate bite resistance, which means that they don't bite too hard to play with their siblings. When the puppies play, if one hits another too hard, the receiver will yip or snap and stop playing. The chomping puppy might not want to stop playing, so he learns to reduce the severity of his bite. Puppies also learn bite resistance from their mother, particularly as she begins to wean them. Puppies are now learning to share with their fellow pups. They learn about resource rivalry, such as with toys or with their mother's milk. There are valuable social lessons that are crucial at this age, which is why it is valuable never to take the puppies away from their families too early. Good breeders and rescue groups will be holding puppies with their families for at least eight weeks.

If a mother dog has one puppy in the litter, called a singleton, it is at a disadvantage. He cannot learn bite avoidance very well because he has no brothers or sisters to show him when he bites too hard. This could prove to be a hurdle for you because the pup could be very mouthy. He never has to share or fight for something, so he may find it really upsetting when he unexpectedly doesn't get what he wants when he comes to your home. You're going to have to spend extra time teaching a singleton puppy.

Some people tend to have two puppies or young puppies at the same time. This is definitely attractive, as the puppies are going to spend a lot of time together and be playmates, but it may create a few problems. Puppies raised together may become overly reliant on each other because they spent their time together, particularly if they're packed together, so they don't learn to be alone. And when one of them has to go to the vet or gets to go somewhere without the other, the puppy left behind can become disturbed. Too much reliance is not safe.

Another problem is that as they spend this much time together they are often more closely bonded to each other than to you or to other people in your family. Dogs are most closely bonded to someone who spends much of the time in meaningful interactions. When a puppy spends most of his time with another puppy in a vital socialization period, that's who he's going to be bonding with. You'll probably find that they're not listening to you, particularly if they're older, which will make their training a bigger challenge.

Some littermates can also grow animosity towards each other as they get older. Often, aggression can escalate to a point where it is not healthy or safe to hold both pups together any longer, which is frustrating.

Raising young puppies together can be done, but it takes a lot of effort, time, and commitment. You'll need to make sure each puppy has its own crate and bowl. You have to divide them every day for individual bonding time with you and other members of your family. You're going to have to train them separately and take turns on journeys and adventures. With all you need to do to get the puppy trained right, the extra effort may prove to be a bigger challenge than you're prepared to face. That's why so many professional trainers don't suggest getting littermates.

A Long Way from Wolves

In the past, commonly held belief has been that dogs have evolved from wolves. Recent work has cast some doubt on this. The more we know about dogs, the more we understand that their history might not be as closely associated with wolves as we believed before.

Whether or not the dogs started out as wolves, they are now a long, long way from Canis lupus. Can you imagine a pack of pugs pulling a caribou down? It's not possible. Humans have transformed dogs, for better or worse, into the household animals that we know and love today.

Why is it important to understand that? And if you think your dog is acting like a wolf, and you try to react accordingly, you're going to be a long way off base. Wolves are pack animals. A pack has a traditional family made up of a breeding pair and its offspring.

Experts used to believe that dogs were social animals, but when they researched village dogs all over the world, they began to understand that this was not likely to have been the case. Village dogs are dogs that may once have been owned by people but have come been abandoned or are descendants of previously owned dogs.

They're often claimed by local people who feed them sometimes, but they're not in-home pets like the dog you brought around.

These dogs have fallen into a natural environment, living near dumps and in cities where they eat. They're not forming groups. Instead, they establish transient friendships, often teaming up with one or two other dogs for a short time and then moving on. Males don't help with the rearing of pups. Dogs of the village don't team up to play together. Instead, they're just scavengers. It's not in the best interest of a scavenger to team up with friends.

People who want to handle their dogs like wolves are barking up the wrong tree. For instance, your dog growls at you when you reach for his collar, so you think he's jockeying for an alpha role. You turn him upside down in an "alpha roll" and catch him until he ends up struggling. This is a huge mistake. A dog may rumble at a collar grab because the action has been associated with a bad experience or because it is scared. Now that you've put your dog into a terrifying place and held him there, you've persuaded him that he's been right all along! Hands around his head are very frightening to him. Your dog will growl at you next time. What you assumed was a rank-and-file game was actually something else, and now you've got a bigger problem on your side.

Your dog knows you're not a wolf or a goat. You don't look or smell like a dog, so pretending to behave like one is only going to annoy or launch him. Your dog won't understand the message you're trying to send, so you may have some serious issues with your delivery.

Early Training and Socialization Benefits

The earlier a dog can actually train, the better. You're trying to avoid bad habits from forming and being entrenched. If you socialize a puppy correctly during its vital socialization phase (up to around sixteen weeks of age), you can help avoid severe behavioral problems later.

You should start training your puppy as early as you get him home. This also refers to juvenile and adult dogs. It's not too late to begin a dog's training. Some people are concerned that their puppies are too young to start, or that their adult dogs are too mature. That is not the case either.

It is true that your puppy will not be allowed to attend team training until all of his vaccinations have been completed, depending on the class. Although you don't have to wait for a class — start practicing at home. Puppies are clean slates, so they seem to learn very easily.

Older breeds, however, aren't that far behind. They may already have some problems you want to change, but they do have a much longer attention span than easily distracted puppies. When you show your older dog how much fun constructive training can be, he's going to become a great student.

CHAPTER THREE

INTERACTING WITH YOUR DOG

In order to educate your dog effectively, you need to connect with him. It sounds easy, but it's not always easy to interact with animals who don't think like we do.

The most common issues between dogs and humans are due to faulty communication. You try to get Fido off the sofa, but he feels the sofa is a comfortable place to peek out the window. You want him to potty outside, but he assumes you're going to let him out to catch squirrels. You're expecting one thing to happen, but your dog may have a totally different idea.

You may think that what you're showing your dog is crystal clear, but he really doesn't know what you're doing. Dogs do not speak English. They can learn your own vocabulary, but you have to teach them. You need to connect with him in words he can understand. So if you say, "Fido, come on!" and he's not running to you, it's not shocking. Repeating the lesson over and over again won't help him learn more easily. Saying it louder or in a more serious voice doesn't help either. He can hear you, but he really doesn't understand what you mean. You've got to teach him to understand what "Fido, come on!" implies. This book is going to help you!

You don't need to scream at your dog or use a harsh tone of voice to succeed. Who wants to scream at their dog all the time? It's just not important, particularly if you're using positive training methods. You could whisper your cues, and he would respond happily.

First, Get the Behavior, Then Add the Signal

Because dogs don't understand your verbal language, it's more important to teach the dog to do the behavior first before placing a verbal mark on it. If you will be going to give your dog a verbal cue when you're first teaching actions, it just cripples the situation and may confuse your dog. However, you are going to want to talk to your dog— it's a natural thing you want to do! Just note that, before you teach him, your words mean very little to your dog.

When you have a stable pattern, you can add a cue to it. It's going to take a lot of repetitions for your dog to realize that when he hears a signal, he's going to have to perform an action. It's harder for dogs to know verbal cues, so it'll take him a while to link them to the appropriate actions. That doesn't mean you're going to perform dull, repetitive drills when you're practicing. Training sessions should be very short— only a couple of minutes at a time. You want to have your dog panting for more, you don't want to annoy him because he's losing interest.

Using Appropriate Cues to Achieve the Best Results

Here are some things to bear in mind when interacting with your dog:

- Keep cues brief so they'll be easier for your dog to grasp. Saying, "Come on!" is more potent than saying," Come over here!" Use one cue to mean one move. If you're using Cue Down because you want your dog to stop jumping on you, don't use Down to tell him to lay down on the ground. It's too hard for your dog. How is he meant to know which Down you're talking about?

- Be consistent with your indicators. If you ask, "Come on!" once upon a time, and then, "Come here!" another day, and then, "Come on!" you're always going to make it harder for your dog to know what you want.

Be sure that everyone who communicates with your dog, such as other family members, uses the same signals.

- Please use a polite voice. Many folks make the error of delivering every cue in a stringent "no-nonsense" voice, but this is not appropriate and may make it much harder for a timid or nervous dog to train. Dogs don't comprehend your words, but they understand your sound. If you say all your cues in a stern voice, your dog may interpret it to mean you're unhappy with it. Even cheerful, bouncy dogs don't have to be taught with a voice like a military drill teacher. Save your growly voice for when your dog does something very bad because if you train your dog, those times will be few and far between!

It's also helpful to use your dog's name right in front of a signal, such as "Fido, stay" or "Fido, down." It can be particularly useful if you have more than one dog and you need to get the attention of a specific dog. Bear in mind, though, that if you don't assign an action to the dog's name, then the name itself doesn't mean anything except to get the dog's interest and point out that you're talking to him.

For instance, in the dog-supply store, you see a grumpy-looking woman with a bouncy Boxer puppy growling at the end of her leash. She calls out, "Buster! Buster! Buster! Buster! Buster! BUSTER, man! BUSTER! Buster!" This is a name, not an act. What does the dog want to do? If the dog has not been taught specifically to do something with the sound of his name, then saying it over and over again is not effective or communicative.

Now assume, for instance, that the owner had told Buster that he should look at her when he heard his name. That would be a nice way to get the puppy's attention and to suggest that his name would mean anything to him.

If you need a cue, just try to say it once. Repeating this isn't going to help your dog follow the cue faster, so you're only going to show him that you're going to say it a dozen times before you expect him to react. It can be a very tough habit for people to break. If you want your dog to react for the first time that you're asking him to do something, you just have to test the action once.

THE BODY TELLS A TALE

If you want to really understand what your dog is telling you, his body language will tell you all about it. Dogs have a dynamic, broad body language vocabulary; this is how they interact best with each other. Dogs know what a nice dog is doing, what it sounds like, and how it behaves. They even identify an enemy dog in the same way. Dogs indicate by their body language when terrified. By signaling with the body language, a dog may disperse a potentially stressful situation and stop combat. Through better knowledge of the body language of a dog, you can understand your dog better.

Ears

When the ears of a dog lie flat, it can imply fear. Forward ears show curiosity or excitement. Remember that certain dogs have ears that don't give them a lot of speech. Cocker Spaniels, for instance, have stunning, long ears that normally lie flat and do not stand upright.

Eyes

A gentle, sweet smile suggests kindness or contentment. Your dog's eyes may be squinted. If your dog looks at you in a friendly or warning face, it's all right. Many people fear that if a dog looks at them in the eyes that it's a threat or a dog is simply showing itself. It's scarcely is! Your dog is probably only making friendly communication or trying to interpret your own language. Eye contact is a sign of boldness, which is not the same thing as hostility. This is why timid or nervous dogs often pull away from you.

Mouth

Some dogs laugh, and that's exactly what you think it is — a sign of excitement. A tight, closed lip is a sign of stress. The lips can be drawn back at the corners. Depending on the situation, panting can indicate stress. A dog who's been playing is going to bark, so that doesn't mean it's mad, but a dog that's scared of thunderstorms is always going to bark when the storm starts. Dogs can pant if they're in pain. However still, if a dog is panting and closes its mouth, there may be an increase in stress. For instance, if a dog is breathing heavily at the vet's office and unexpectedly stops as the vet's technician approaches with the thermometer, the dog's stress has just intensified.

When a dog tells you or another animal to steer clear, his lips can move forward over his teeth to make them look puffy. His lips may even curl up in a snarl and withdraw to reveal his teeth; this may be followed by a groan. It's separate from a submissive smile, which is frequently mistaken for a snarl. In a submissive expression, the lips of the dog draw up vertically to reveal the front teeth. It's often followed by a subservient body posture — a curved back, a short, wagging tail, occasionally looking away, and squinty eyes.

Tail

The tail curled under is a symbol of terror. A wagging tail is frequently mistaken for a sign of kindness, but this may be a serious error. Just because a dog is wagging its tail doesn't mean that it's social or that it wants you to pet it. A tail that is very low and shaking quickly can give rise to stress or anxiety and can also give rise to excitement. The tail, which is held very high and wagging, shows high enthusiasm. The dog might be excited to welcome you, or he might be irritated and may contemplate lunging and even biting. Generally speaking, a mid-level or low, frilly tail wag is a symbol of joy or friendliness. Some dogs are so incredibly happy that their tails go flying around in wide circles.

Overall Body Posture

A dog's overall body posture will tell you a lot about his thoughts and what he is feeling. A dog that puts most of its weight on his forelegs is attempting to increase the distance between himself and something. He may be confused or frightened. When his weight is positioned forward, he's trying to reduce the gap. He's curious or willing to do something. For instance, a puppy who is unsure of a tall man may lean backwards, away from a man. If he feels that the guy is fine, he's going to lean or step towards him. When a dog is tense, he's going to move his weight back and forth. At the same time, he may be scared but interested.

A curved body pose suggests friendliness or pacification. Many dogs appear to wiggle and wag with their whole body! When a dog lifts his paw it can indicate peace of mind and could be an invitation to play. When a dog drops his head and bends his knees, but the back of the dog stays straight, this is considered a play bow. It's an open invite to play, and a way for a dog to show that it's not a threat.

When a dog drops his head, tightens his body, and puts on a hard-hitting "lock and load" face, his aim is to attack. It doesn't actually mean that the dog is going to bite, but it obviously wants you to leave. He could escalate to a bite if pushed. You can see the fur growing on the back of his neck or all the way down his back. This is called "piloerection."

Signs of Stress

Just like a dog's body language shows you if he's relaxed or violent, it can tell you whether he's anxious or afraid. Those are vital signs you need to know. If your dog shows signs of nervousness or anxiety when you are exercising, for instance, you will need to interrupt your training session and fix your dog's discomfort. It's a lot tougher for a dog to know when he's mad. Imagine trying to learn a difficult math equation if you were scared — it would be challenging! If you want to have a successful training session, it is better to understand the canine signs of anxiety so that you can track your dog's state of mind. Stress indicators are also important for learning as you socialize a young puppy, as well as guiding your dog to navigate its life.

If your dog displays one or two of the following features, it doesn't necessarily imply he's anxious or afraid. Take into account his body language as a whole and understand the context. For instance, if you take your dog to a pet-supply store and he yawns a little and licks his lips, but runs brightly and pulls you to explore, he's probably excited.

However, if he yawns, licks his lips, folds his tail, and comes and presses against you, then he's stressed.

There are signs of stress to check for:

- Licking lips
- Yawning
- Cowering
- Trembling
- Whining
- Shaking off (akin to what dogs do when they're wet, however, in this case they're dry)
- Tucking tail
- Turning away, resisting, trying to get away
- Flattening ears
- Wet pawprints (dogs sweat via their paw pads)

Sometimes a dog displays some conduct that is out of context. It's a usual action, but it's strange regarding the situation. This is called the "displacement signal" or the "cutoff signal" and may suggest stress. Your friend, for instance, brings her new puppy to meet your dog. When the puppy enters the house, your dog runs over to meet him. Suddenly, the puppy starts to sniff the ground. It's not odd for a puppy to sniff on the floor, but it seems to be a strange priority for another dog to sniff into his private space. Sniffing is a signal of displacement. The puppy could demonstrate to your dog that it is not a threat by resisting direct eye contact. He may also mean that he was irritated by your dog's vexatious greeting.

Your Body Language

Just as your dog interacts with you through body language, your body language sends messages to your dog. Sometimes you may send messages that you don't really say. For instance, if you bend or loom over a dog, you might unintentionally threaten him. Most dogs won't mind it at all, however, sensitive or nervous dogs may be afraid.

Your body language will have an impact on your training. If you bend down at your knees and call your dog to come to you, he might come, but he will be sitting at a distance from you, so you won't be standing over him. When you bend your knees and bend down to call him, he will come more eagerly because you have lowered your body and are less intimidating.

Whether you're upset or sad, the vocabulary of your body changes. Just make sure that when you train your dog, you are in a good mood and full of patience; otherwise, you will feel irritated. Your body may be stiffer, your hands will clench, your jaw may clench then relax, and your voice may sound different. You might think you're behaving the same way you naturally do, but your dog is very perceptive and even notices the slightest changes. Your dog may be less likely to answer your signals if you are nervous or upset. He could even start running around and acting crazy, trying to relieve the stress! This is probably only going to make you nervous, and it ends up being a boring training session.

It's very assertive to stare a dog in the eyes, and some dogs may find it a challenge. This can be especially frustrating with kids. Many kids like to clutch a dog's nose, get close, and look in his eyes. We say it's for affection, but don't let that happen! While some dogs will accept this, some won't. And in this situation, the proximity of the dog to the child's face is highly dangerous. And if the dog doesn't seem to mind, kids still don't realize what one dog likes and another dog doesn't. If your child is going to want to get too close to a dog that is less than friendly there may be an accident.

Because dogs are so tuned to body language, it's easier to teach them hand signals. It is simpler for them to learn hand signals or other visual cues than it is for them to understand verbal cues. They can study verbal cues, of course, but it tends to take a little longer.

It is crucial to be constant when using hand signals or other visual cues with your dog, much like with certain dimensions of dog training. If you step down with your hand pointing when you teach your dog to Down, but then one day you hold your hand on your side, your dog can not respond. He's not rebellious, he's just confused. He's discovered that your hand pointing downwards means that you want him to lie down, but you didn't make that move. That doesn't mean that you just have to make dramatic hand gestures to make your dog work. You can "fade" hand gestures to make them smaller, you just need to do it slowly.

Dog's Senses

The senses of a dog are far more pronounced than that of a human. This is why your dog is so good at reading the language of your body. This also confirms why dogs can be distracted during training or when you take them for a stroll or when you introduce them to new places. They can do things you can't do!

The All-Knowing Nose

A dog's sense of smell is unusual. Experts have not been able to determine how strong it is, although they believe that it is 10,000 to 100,000 times more intense than ours. Pups have up to 300 million olfactory (scent) receptors in their noses. We've got about six million of them. Dogs have a large part of their brains devoted to odor analysis— about 40 percent more than we do.

We smell and breathe from the same channels in our noses as we inhale. As dogs inhale, a fold of tissue within their noses separates the air into two pathways: one for sensing, and the other for breathing. Scientists have estimated that about 12 percent of the air goes to the recessed portion in the back of the dog's nose, which is devoted to smelling. The remainder of it goes to the lungs.

When we exhale, we push the air out the way it came in— through a single direction. When the dogs exhale, the air travels through the slits on the sides of their noses. When the air blows out, fresh smells flow through the dog's nose. It also helps a dog to sniff almost endlessly.

As if this wasn't enough on its own to make them magnificent smelling machines, dogs have an organ included in part of their anatomy that we don't have. It's named the Jacobson's organ. This is at the base of the dog's nasal passage, and it detects pheromones, which are the chemicals that animals emit to attract other animals, particularly their mates. The pheromone molecules that Jacobson's organ detects do not interact with other odor molecules. The Jacobson organ has its own nerves, which connect to a portion of the brain devoted to the examination of pheromones.

No wonder the dogs are so distracted by the smells! They are very good at smelling because of their anatomy. Several breeds and individual dogs are better at scenting than others, but all dogs have a far superior scent ability than we do. Dogs excel in scent games, such as tracking and K9 Nose Work ®. They also help people by participating in search and rescue, discovering corpses, and more. Some have been taught to spot termites, bed bugs, and even cancer.

The Eyes

We used to believe that dogs could only see in black and white, but new research suggests differently. Dogs likely have some sort of color vision. The perception of color by the eye is based on the presence of cone photoreceptors in the retina of the eye. The photoreceptors of the cone function under bright light. The central region of the human retina consists of 100 percent cone photoreceptors, although only about 20 percent of the photoreceptors in the same region in dogs are cone photoreceptors. And while we can see a wide variety of colors, dogs can see only a handful. Scientists performed behavioral experiments on dogs that showed that dogs could distinguish between red and blue but had trouble telling the difference between red and green.

Where the eyes are positioned on the head defines what kind of peripheral vision an animal has as well as the extent of the visual field that both eyes can see at one time. Dogs' eyes are on the sides of their heads, which means they have a visual field of 240 degrees, while humans have a visual field of 200 degrees.

Binocular vision is used to judge range. Dogs have about half the binocular vision as humans do. Dogs have stronger peripheral vision than we do, but they must be nearer to objects than humans to see them properly.

Can Dogs Hear?

Puppies are born deaf. They can't open their ears until they're around two weeks old. Some dogs have fluffy ears, and can be short or long. Some of them have pricked up ears. No matter what shape or size, there are around eighteen muscles in the ear that move in multiple directions to help the dog hear sounds. Dogs' ears will operate independently of each other. Dogs can detect sounds at a much higher frequency than we do.

The ear canal of a dog is distinct from that of a human. People have ear canals which are parallel to the ear drum. The ear canal is L-shaped in dogs. It's horizontal towards the jaw and then it takes a 90 degree turn to rotate horizontally towards the ear drum. This structure makes it impossible to inspect the ear canal without specialized equipment. It also leaves the ear a host for bacterial and yeast infections, particularly in droopy-eared dogs, where the ear flap covers the ear canal and creates a moist setting.

Taste and Feel

Dogs don't get as many taste buds as we do, which means they can't taste as many spices as we do. It can explain why certain dogs want to have plenty to eat! Dogs can taste spicy, salty, sour, and bitter tastes, but they smell more than they taste. Their strong sense of smell compensates a little for their lack of taste buds.

Dogs have a strong sense of touch. Mothers instantly kiss their newborns, and very young puppies stay huddled together for comfort. They have touch-sensitive fur called vibrissae above the lips, on the muzzle, and below the jaw. Vibrissae can sense the movement of air. The whole body of a dog, including its paws, has touch-sensitive nerve endings.

Because a dog can sense the touch doesn't mean that he finds all the petting pleasing. Individual dogs can form individual tastes. One dog, for instance, would love to have you scratch behind his ears, while another might be repositioning himself so you can scratch his back. Many dogs just don't like petting at all. They may not be inclined because they didn't get the right opportunity as puppies, or it could just be a personal preference.

CHAPTER FOUR

EMPHASIZE THE POSITIVE!

Positive science-based training is very effective. It works for all sorts of dogs, including those considered "arrogant" or "difficult." It works well with nervous and timid dogs. It also works for large dogs, little dogs, puppies, adults, bouncy pets, and couch potatoes— because it meets the basic laws of learning. You can train any species with mindfulness. Most wild animal trainers use positive reinforcement to get big, potentially harmful animals to perform their activities. If elephants were trained to offer their feet willingly for care, or if they can train tigers to sit patiently for blood draws, then you can train your dog without using pressure or bullying.

Here are some of the rewards of positive training:

- You wouldn't have to rely on physical prowess to train your dog. It doesn't allow you to place your dog in a spot, or push or pull it to do what you want to do. It opens learning to a much broader range of people with various physical abilities and also allows them to train bigger dogs. It also ensures that your children can train your dog (with oversight).
- This is productive. The sessions are very short with constructive preparation. A few minutes is all you need for a session. Short lessons work best for dogs, particularly young puppies with limited attention spans! It's perfect for someone with a busy schedule too. You can always arrange a session within a few minutes, and if you do that a couple of times a day, you'll see great progress.
- It's delivering immediate results. The dog will look forward to the training sessions and become more loyal to you, and you'll be able to teach him quicker.
- You're going to get your dog to want to work for you, rather than be afraid to disobey you. This is forging a good friendship.
- It's really fun! The coaching of your dog does not have to be a difficult task. By using constructive methods, both you and your dog will enjoy the learning experience.

Just because you're using positive training methods doesn't mean that you let your dog get away with whatever it wants. "Good" does not mean "lenient." You should set your dog's rules and boundaries. You should have reasonable expectations of his actions and teach him to function within these guidelines. You can do so completely, and you can still practice positively. You don't have to be strict with your dog before you teach him what you want him to know.

Understanding the Scientific Principles of Training

Positive training approaches in this book are focused on research. They are based on the theory of learning from the work of psychologists, behaviorists, and more. If you've taken a Psychology class, you might be familiar with these concepts. Because these methods are based on science, they have been subjected to scientific scrutiny time and time again. They're working. They're working with every animal with a nervous system.

Scientists have used these training techniques for laboratory animals— if the animal completes the task right, it gets a slice of food. The animal continues to perform the role more often.

Wild animal and marine mammal trainers are using these methods. They instruct performance behaviors, but more and more, they also train animals to perform husbandry behaviors that make it easier to care for the animals and to attend to their medical care. Instances include teaching a whale to roll up so that a doctor can conduct an ultrasound, teaching a wolf to stand still to seek care on an infected leg, and teaching a gorilla to raise the arm willingly for an insulin shot.

Animal owners are still using these methods. They're focused on birds, horses, pigs, and even cats. Although there is a lot of science related to canine behavior, you first need to recognize classical and operant conditioning to train your dog.

Classical Conditioning

Classical conditioning is the method of associating a neutral stimulus with an unconscious response before the stimulus activates the reaction. Neutral stimulation is something that means nothing. The dog has nothing to do with it. The unconscious reaction is something that the animal does automatically without thinking about. For instance, if a dog sees food, it will start to salivate. It's an involuntary response. The dog doesn't think about salivating; it just does it.

Ivan Pavlov, a Russian physiologist, became the first to note the concept of classical conditioning. He studied digestion in dogs when he found that the dogs would begin to salivate when his assistant entered the room. At that point, the dogs had not been given food, but they were already salivating. He argued that salivation had become a trained reaction rather than an unconscious one. The dogs started salivating once they saw the assistant through whom they had learned to expect food.

So Pavlov experimented with some other neutral stimuli. He would trigger a metronome right before offering food to dogs. The metronome means almost nothing to the dogs, after many rehearsals of the metronome just before the dogs got food, the dogs started to salivate at the sound of the metronome. The dogs had known that the metronome sound meant that food was coming. The stimulus was no longer neutral; it was what was called a "conditioned stimulus." The conditioned stimulus now created a "conditioned response"— salivation.

You actually did a lot of classic conditioning without even knowing it. The very first time your dog saw a leash it didn't really mean anything to him. He may have sniffed it or been skeptical about it, but he was just examining it. That was a neutral stimulus.

Differently, your dog would be excited about getting to go out for a walk. His enthusiasm was an unintended reply.

Taking him out on the leash many times will make the relationship with the leash improve. After a while, when he sees the rope he may jump with enthusiasm or begin to bark. He came to link the leash with the exercises. The leash is now a programmed stimulus, and his anticipation was a conditioned reaction to seeing the leash. The leash means walking around!

Operant Conditioning

Operant conditioning is the method of modifying the response of the animal to a certain stimulus by controlling the effects that occur right after the reaction. Behavior will be either praised or punished. Behavior that is rewarded has increased intensity. Behavior that is punished is reduced in intensity.

There are four primary organizational conditioning quadrants: positive reinforcement, positive punishment, negative reinforcement, and negative punishment. Since these are psychological terms, the words "positive" and "negative" have different meanings. In this case, they do not mean "good" and "evil." Rather, "positive" means "apply" and "negative" means "delete."

Positive reinforcement — Something beneficial is introduced after a behavior that causes behavior to improve. If you call your dog to come and handle him when he does, he's likely to come back to you when you call him again. An illustration among people is that if you complete a project at work, and your employer gives you a bonus, you're likely to finish more projects.

Positive punishment — Something harmful is applied to the behavior that allows the behavior to decrease. When you call your dog to you, and when he arrives, you scream at him or plunk him in the bathtub because he hates the bathtub, he's less likely to approach you when you call again. In the same vein, if you stay late to finish a job at work, and your boss screams at you for overtime, you're less likely to stay late to work on projects in the future.

Negative Reinforcement — Something bad is eliminated after the activity has increased. If there's a thorn in your dog's paw, and you ask him to come and remove the thorn and make his paw less painful, he's more likely to come to you when you call again. If your supervisor is continuously shouting at you before you complete the job, you're more likely to finish the tasks quickly in the future.

Negative Punishment — Something good is eliminated after conduct and behavior is reduced. If your dog is happily chewing on the bone, and you call him to come and take the bone away from him, he's less likely to come to you when you call again.

Reinforcement, whether added or removed (positive or negative), often enhances behavior. Punishment, whether added or removed (positive or negative), often decreases behavior.

Positive training usually requires the most work of these four quadrants— positive reinforcement and negative punishment. When a dog exhibits the behavior you want, and you want to raise the frequency, you praise it— positive reinforcement. For instance, every time your dog sits down, you pet him, so he starts to sit down more often. You gave him attention to sitting down, which is rewarding to him.

When the dog does something you don't like, and you want it to decrease in frequency, you can take the reward away, and the conduct will decrease— negative reinforcement. For instance, if your dog jumps on you, and you ignore him absolutely, and you don't pay him any attention at all, he stops jumping on you. You've taken your attention away, and his conduct is no longer rewarding.

Training Behaviors Step-by-Step

A cue is the word or physical gesture that you would use to ask the dog to perform the action. To get a dog to do a task when you point it out, you have to demonstrate the task first. There are some general steps that need to be taken to get a dog to execute a behavior consistently.

Step 1: Get the Behavior

There are several exciting ways to get a dog to obey, including luring / targeting, grooming, capturing, and modeling.

Luring / Targeting

Luring and targeting are hands-off strategies for directing a dog through behavior. For instance, you could use a treat in your hand to persuade a dog to lie down. When you lower the treat, he bends his nose to follow it, and then his body follows. Or, you could teach a dog to touch his nose to your hand, making your hand a focus. You will teach your dog to come to you, get on and off the bed, and get in and out of the vehicle by watching the direction of your hand.

Luring and targeting are perhaps the most commonly used behavioral strategies. They can also be the strongest, depending on the dog's behavior. They usually work really well with most dogs.

In order to attract the dog to work, the lure has to be really persuasive. If you use a boring lure, it won't be followed by a dog. So if you try to lure your dog during a training session, and he keeps giving up after a few sniffs or ignores you altogether, it's time to find a more effective lure.

During lure training, it is important to lose your lure very quickly, or you and your dog can become dependent on the lure. For instance, after you've successfully persuaded your dog with a treat to lie down three times, you're going to do it without having a treat in your pocket. You're going to hold your hand the same way you did before, as if you were always holding a treat. Pretend that you already have the treat in your pocket and use your empty hand to attract the dog the same way you did before. Your dog is supposed to follow your empty hand down. When the dog lays down, you should "mark" the action (with a click or verbal marker, which is explained later in this book) and then treat it. This treat is his reward for the success of his actions. You're going to lose the lure long before you wean the dog away from incentives.

It's not a trick to fool your puppy. Dogs have an incredible sense of smell. Your dog knows there's no treat with you. What he's picking is your hand gesture. You're basically giving your dog a hand gesture by putting your hand down.

If you have a treat in your hand every time you ask your dog to go down, he will know that he can lie down only when you have a treat in your hand. Some owners remain dependent on luring with treatments because they are concerned that their dogs will not pay attention to them unless they have treats in their hands. If you hold a lure in your hand for too long, this fear might come true! Be sure to lose your attention easily when you lure.

Shaping

Shaping involves developing behavior by improving progressive parts of behavior. For instance, if you were shaping the cue, Settle on your dog's bed, you would first reinforce the dog to look at his bed, then to move to his bed, then to sniff his bed, then to put one paw on the bed, then to put two paws on the bed, then to put three or four paws on the bed, and finally to lie down on the bed. The target is for the dog to step towards the bed and lay down on it. Through shaping, you reinforce all the small pieces of the action that make up your target actions.

Shaping has a lot of advantages. It encourages a dog to always pay attention to your marker (click or verbal marker) so that he knows what action you're rewarding for. Dogs also seem to hold shaped behaviors longer, perhaps because they need to figure out the process. Have you ever asked someone to drive you somewhere, for instance, and then expect you to know the way when you drive there yourself? You can hesitate a few turns or get stuck on a few streets before you reach your destination. Yet as you drive to places of your own, you know the right route. You had to do it yourself to know how to get there.

Shaping is really useful for a dog who may be too afraid to get close to you for luring. You may have a tasty meatball in your hand to tempt your dog to behave, but if the dog is scared of you, the meatball might not be enough. Shaping helps you to interact with a dog that doesn't feel comfortable getting next to you. It, in effect, will help create a positive bond as it will earn several rewards during the training sessions. Your training sessions will be a good experience for him.

Shaping is also an excellent training method for teaching behaviors that a dog would not normally do. A dog can easily pick up a tennis ball, but what about your car keys? You could shape your dog to bring your keys, remote control, laundry items, or other objects to you.

Shaping is a perfect method for teaching service-dog habits, such as turning on and off lights, opening and closing doors, and even helping to make a bed.

Capturing

Capturing is a technique of marking and strengthening the behavior of a dog on its own without lures. For instance, when your dog lies down, he often crosses his front paws, and you think it's cute, so you want to put it on the cue. You will be able to mark and reward the action every time he does it on his own. That behavior will improve, and your dog will begin to lie down and cross his paws more often. If the action is consistent, you can put it on the cue to do something when you point it out. Capturing is a perfect way to capture rare, unique activities that your dog does, something that would be hard to lure. For instance, you might catch a dog shaking off after a bath, tilting its head, or stretching.

Modeling

Modeling is a technique that uses physical coercion to get a dog to behave. This is a form that we do not usually use. It's not necessary because you can get behavior by using other, easier methods. Why drive your dog back down to lie down when you can easily get him to do it on his own?

Modeling can also be complicated for a lot of people. Imagine a little woman getting a fully grown mastiff to sit by pushing her back down! It doesn't engage the dog either— you're doing all the work for him. It's not the best training technique for timid or nervous dogs as they may be more scared by the physical handling of their bodies.

Step 2: Note the Behavior and Reward It

Marker training is an incredibly effective form of positive reinforcement. You mark the moment the dog demonstrates the action you like, usually with a clicker. A clicker is a box-shaped instrument that produces a "click" sound when you press it to one side. The short sound is unique and thus quick for a dog to detect and to identify. You accompany every mark with a reward, therefore a click is a promise of reward. Once your dog knows that every time he sees a marker he gets a treat, and he will continue to try to "see" the marker noise.

You may also use a verbal marker, but to be precise, it must be a very short term. It's meant to be a word that you don't always use in casual conversation so you don't frustrate your dog.

Something such as "good dog" is too long to be an effective marker. Think of all the things that your dog might do by the time you start the "Better" and end the "Bad."

Furthermore, recognition is not the same thing as a marker. You use a marker to tell a dog that he did something you like. When the dog demonstrates the action, you use praise as a reward.

There are a lot of good reasons to use a marker.

- Communication is very simple and accurate. This marks the exact moment that the dog exhibits the action you like.
- The clickers are different. They don't sound the same as other sounds so you can easily identify your dog by clicking.
- This is true. The sound is the same every time, particularly if you use a clicker.
- This is non-judgmental. It's a neutral tone.
- It's transferable. As soon as the dog recognizes the sound of the marker, it means he did what you wanted, then everyone will use it to tell the dog the same thing. This is especially

helpful if you have more than one person in your family who needs your dog to work for him or her.

You need perfect timing to use the marker efficiently. Whether you've never trained a dog before, or whether you've used this kind of training previously, be gentle with yourself! You're learning a new ability. Like with every other new talent, it will take time to learn how to do it. Your timing can be too slow at first, or even too fast, but with practice, you're going to get better.

Another nice thing about marker training is that even though you're a rookie, you're not going to make errors that will set back your training or damage your dog a lot. For punishment-based discipline, punishing the dog at the wrong time may have unintended consequences. Not the case with the teaching of markers! You can mark a little early or late and not get the exact behavior you expected, but you'll be able to correct it easily with a few more clicks. No harm has been done.

Below are some tips on the proper use of a clicker.

- Don't point it at your puppy. He's not a remote control!
- Click for actions just once. It's a marker, and you're only marking a similar activity once. If your dog does something

very good, you only click once, but if you like, you can give him a better reward or a few rewards.

- Only use the clicker to label actions, not for other items. When a dog discovers that a click means a reward is coming, he may get really excited about the click sound. It could be tempting, though, to use the clicker to get your dog's attention or to use the sound to get him to run to you if you don't know where he is in the house or yard. When you do so, the strength of the click as a marker has just been weakened.

- Always after clicking offer a treat. And if you make a mistake and press at the wrong time, you need to praise your puppy. It's not the fault of your dog that you got it wrong. If you missed the reward because you clicked wrongly, the power of the click will be reduced. When you do it often enough, then your dog may stop paying full attention to the click.

- Because the click shows the action, the action stops. For instance, when you're working on the Down Cue, when your dog lies down, you click, and when your dog gets up, it's okay. You've already marked down, so it's all right if he gets up to get his treat.

Step 3: Add a Cue

When the behavior is consistent, which means that the dog performs the behavior on a daily basis, it's time to add a cue (the word or physical signal you would use to ask the dog to perform the behavior).

How don't we first introduce the cue? How don't we say "down" and then coax a dog to the down position? Since it's not that easy for dogs to think that way. Note, they're not speaking English. Saying "under" does not mean anything to them. Repeating it over and over is not helpful either. When someone says something to you in a foreign language that you don't know, does it help you to understand it if they repeat it over and over? If they scream at you? Of course it's not. It's not going to support your dog. That's why, first, we teach actions, and then mark it with a cue.

With stationary habits, such as Sit, Down, and Settle, it's helpful to teach a release warning. This is a signal to your dog that it's all right to get up. Otherwise, is he supposed to stay sitting forever? And does he just get up whenever he wants? By teaching a release cue, you're going to help him stay longer, and be more consistent. You should use the same release cue for each exercise as it still means the same behavior— your dog doesn't have to hold the pose anymore. Use a phrase that you don't always use in casual conversations, such as "Ok!" "Free" or "Lock." The original phrase doesn't matter so long as you comply with its usage.

Step 4: Train to Fluency

Once you have a cue behavior, it's time to practice your fluency. This means that you're going to need to teach your dog to do so with challenges, in different situations, and under different circumstances. This doesn't really do you a lot of good if your dog just plays in your living room for you. However, if that's the only place where you practice, that's also the only place where your dog's actions can be done consistently.

You show your dog how to sit-stay at home, for instance. You take him to the park and point him out, "Stop, Stay." He rests, but then jumps right up and begins pursuing a squirrel. This may be distracting, but it's not odd at all. You've never trained your dog to sit-stay outside with all its scents and sounds, let alone squirrels.

This can happen with house-training too. That you taught your dog not to kill in your own home doesn't mean that he knows not to murder in other people's homes. So, if you take your dog to a relative's house during the holidays, he might be peeing on the carpet even if he hasn't done it in your house for some time. Although his peeing may be due to stress or excitement, it may also be due to lack of training at various places.

You work slowly to teach fluency actions. Start with a few distractions and then slowly add more and more. You will need to keep the training sessions short. If you consider your dog suffering, you're probably going to get out too soon. Back up to the last move that your dog has been good, practice more at that point, and then try to make it harder again.

Be quick to introduce distractions to your workout. Once you start working on a behavior for the first time, you start with very few distractions. Train in a quiet environment that your dog is comfortable with, like your family room. When the conduct is stable, add a few distractions to your training sessions. Depending on the activity you're focusing on, you may be moving around, going farther away from your dog, shifting your training spot, losing items, having other people walking around, having other dogs around, and the like. Only slowly introduce the distractions.

For instance, if you're working on Sit-Stay, you're going to move one pace away to make sure your dog keeps the spot, then two paces, then three. You wouldn't have gone from sitting right next to your dog

Puppy Training For Beginners

to being in the house. This would probably be too much for your dog, and he will break the position.

Depending on your dog's age and temperament, fluency training can take time. It's usual! Rushing him isn't going to be effective. You want him to show that he is successful rather than that he is ineffective. Young puppies don't have much attention span, so they're easily distracted. Anything as tiny as a ladybug could prove to be a nuisance for a puppy compared to an older dog. Some breeds, such as bouncy boxers or jumping Labradors, are by nature active. Keep your patience and go as fast as your dog can make progress. Your preparation is worth your efforts! By gradually increasing diversions and introducing new settings, you're going to have a dog that can work for you in any situation.

Think of service dogs who need to be effective in busy settings, such as hospitals, or emotionally fraught situations, such as hospice bereavement groups. Search and rescue dogs will work in often dangerous circumstances, including noisy sounds and unpleasant smells. Patrol dogs have to work in a number of environments, from classrooms to alleys. This level of performance does not happen automatically or overnight. Training habits are needed for fluency so that the dog learns to be reliable under a variety of conditions.

Reward-Based Learning

If you were offered chocolate chip cookies, ice cream, or tiramisu, would you have a preference? Your teeth may be prone to cold, so you won't find the ice cream appealing. You might not like the taste of coffee, so the tiramisu has no appeal. Or maybe you really don't like chocolate, so chocolate-chip cookies wouldn't be of interest to you. Everyone has different tastes when it comes to things they want. Dogs are quite similar.

Not every dog likes to be petted. Many dogs are cool with it, but they just don't like it. Many dogs will do whatever it takes to snuggle with you. Some dogs go nuts for sticks, and they can play fetch for hours at a time. Some dogs just look at you when you throw a ball and never try to chase it. Some dogs are going to eat everything you place in front of them, while others are very picky.

It is really important to know exactly what your dog finds rewarding while using reward-based training. In the eyes of your particular dog, the things you use as incentives must be appealing.

So, what do you think your dog will find appealing? Create a list, according to your dog's preferences. It will help you learn, particularly when it comes to adding distractions or teaching your dog difficult behaviors. Many dogs, for instance, have trouble with Down. If using daily food as a lure doesn't make them lie down, you may need to get a higher-ranked reward on your list.

One of the most popular musings about using incentives for training is, "When will you stop using them?" You will use rewards when you build behavior. When a fluency habit has been learned, it's a safe idea to hold the rewards for a while and then slowly wean your dog away from them. It means that when your dog demonstrates his conduct consistently through obstacles and in various situations, you will begin to wean him away from rewards. Most people want to get rid of the incentives too early, and they find the dog's conduct fails as a result.

There's a big difference between a reward and a bribe. Upon a performance, a reward is given. A bribe is given to get some kind of conduct. You're not trying to cheat your puppy! If you do, it's going to become dependent on that bribe, and you definitely don't want it. You want your puppy to get off the sofa, for instance. You're going to give him the cue "Down!" and he's going to get off the sofa. You're giving him a treat. Yeah, you've given him a hint, he's done the right thing, and he's got a reward.

Take the same situation, only this time you're going to have a treat and reveal it to him, enticing him to get off the sofa. Then you're going to give him the treat. It's a payoff. Do that often enough, and your dog won't get off the sofa when you decide to handle him. You don't want to carry treats around with you all the time just to get your dog to do what you want. You should teach your dog to respond with rewards, not bribes.

Attention and Affection

Many dogs enjoy attention, though not all of them enjoy petting and other physically affectionate movements. For instance, a lot of dogs don't like being petted on the top of their head. This is a fairly assertive move when interpreted by dogs, so many are going to get out of the way or avoid your side. Many dogs don't even care.

When you physically communicate with your dog, what does his body language suggest to you? Is he going stiff? Do his ears lie flat, do his eyes have an expression of concern? Is he turning away from you? Is he fighting? These are all signs that he doesn't enjoy your interaction. At the other side, is he leaning towards you? Does his body feel relaxed? Do his eyes get squinty? These are signs that he loves the contact.

If you want to cuddle with your dog, but your dog doesn't want to cuddle with you, please respect the wishes of your dog. When you force him to tolerate it, he will feel the need to change the way he communicates to you that he doesn't like it. He can start to growl or even snap or bite. This can happen quickly with children who don't know that a dog is unhappy, but it can also happen to adults. Pay attention to the puppy. He's going to tell you if he likes your petting.

If you have a dog who loves physical interaction, learn what he likes best. Does he like a good ear scratch? Belly rub? Chest rub? Choose his preferences to be used as bonuses.

Verbal Praise

While verbal praise is always useful if you don't have a higher value reward with you, although it's not usually as valued by dogs as it is by humans. When you tell a friend how great she is, she's always going to be happy. Your dog will always be happy, but if a choice is made between positive praise and care, the dog will generally prefer the care at any moment.

Please don't be mad. It doesn't mean your dog doesn't love you, and it doesn't mean you're a poor pet owner. When your dog would rather have a treat than hear you speak to him, it's pretty natural. It's very humbling, but it's natural.

In general, if verbal praise is to be effective, it should be enthralling and effective. Get a big deal out of it! Watch out for your dog. Is it offering you a supportive body language in return? Then you're doing the right thing.

Food Incentive

Food is typically a high-value service for any dog. It could be the quickest incentive for teaching behaviors. When you use food, the bits should be small and easy to swallow. What you need is a tiny bite per action. Hard sweets, such as baked cookies, which take a while to chew, are not suitable for training as they can lengthen the training sessions and add too much time between rehearsals.

Treats with heavy odors are more attractive to dogs. If you're practicing at home with a few distractions, you can use your dog's daily kibble to practice if he's working for it. It is a perfect way to control the amount of food you feed your puppy each day and prevent problems with obesity. Get him to work for his food! Just measure what you would normally feed him and use part or all of it in your training sessions during the day. You won't use it all at once because the training sessions should be very short.

Let's assume that you feed your dog 2 cups (453.6 g) of kibble a day. You are currently working on isolation, recall, and settlement preparation. You should use 1 cup (226.8 g) of the kibble during the day for Recall training, 1/2 cup (113.4 g) stuffed in a toy for containment training to keep him occupied and comfortable in his crate, and the last 1/2 cup (113.4 g) stuffed in a toy for a long time.

If you start training in other areas and add distractions, you may have to up the ante with the food. For some dogs, plain kibble can work, but it's going to take a treat that smells stronger for others. For instance, if you take your dog to a training class, you're likely to need a more enticing treat than your dog's usual kibble. There will be a lot of distractions, including other dogs and people, so your dog's kibble may not be as appealing to him in that situation as it is at home.

If you are using dog medications, choose those that are safe. Treats you find in the grocery store, for instance, are mostly full of dyes and sugars. They're not appropriate for training, and they're not a safe option for your dog. Pick a treat with natural ingredients.

Your food incentives may also depend on your training actions and location. For instance, if Sit is a simple habit for your dog to know, a lower-value treat may be used as a reward. If you teach more demanding habits, such as Heel, you might need a higher-value food treat.

When you're practicing in the privacy of your own living room, you might be able to use kibble effectively. If you're in the middle of a busy park, you might need to get higher value rewards to keep your dog's attention.

Which kind of food does your dog enjoy? Some dogs will work for their daily kibble, and some will be picky. Many dogs are enthusiastic for lettuce; some may avoid it entirely. Every dog has its own preferences, so it's going to depend on your dog. It's a misconception that certain dogs are not going to fight for food at all.

Even dogs have to feed. There's a food that's rewarding for every dog. Others may require more detective work than others. Another explanation why a dog may appear unmotivated by food is that if food is left out all day for him (called free food), then food is still available to him, so it doesn't have much power as a reward. It can have an effect on your training ability. Leaving food available all day can also contribute to obesity in dogs if they are not self-regulating effectively.

If you practice with food, you're always going to need something comfortable to keep your food in. You should buy a bait pack which is specially designed to carry the treats when you're in training. You may use a fanny pack or a carpenter's apron as well. A shirt with large pockets will work as well. All that is needed is your ability to reach the treats easily. You must be able to get to the treats easily, without having to search for them.

Toys

Toys can be a fun reward. Many dogs love games, while others are not as interested. Some dogs do love to retrieve toys, while some like to use tug toys. Some dogs will do anything for a ball.

For those who love to use toys as rewards, just bear in mind that training sessions can take longer as you're going to have to encourage playtime with a toy as a reward. This might not be realistic for certain activities or early in the training cycle, when fast repetitions will help your dog learn to behave more quickly.

Please choose healthy toys for your dog. A chew toy that can fit into the dog's entire mouth is not healthy. He could swallow it whole, and he could get it trapped in his throat or digestive tract. Tennis balls are suitable for a lot of dogs, but not dogs who chew on them because the tennis balls will damage their tooth enamel. When your dog likes to chase a tennis ball, that's all right, but he shouldn't sit down with it and chew it like a treat.

Play

Even though you can use toys to play with your puppy, you don't always have to play with a toy. Games, like tracking, hide-and-seek, and remembering, can be enjoyable incentives for certain dogs, and provide a good way to break up a training session if your dog gets upset. When you're playing chase, inspire your dog to chase you, not the other way around. You don't want him to learn by running away from you, but playing a fun game in which he's running towards you will help you teach him a fast come.

Recall games can be fun for active dogs who like to run. When you have more than one person at your side to play, one of you should call your dog to "Come." As the dog runs away from a human, the human takes a step backwards. Finally, you can be in various rooms in your home, or spread out in a fenced yard, with your dog playing in between. Not only is this a challenge, it's also a challenge of preparation. You may also change this game to hide-and-seek, with various people hiding and calling your dog to come and find them.

Just like with toys, playing games will extend your training sessions, but short breaks of play during your training sessions as rewards can be very powerful motivators.

Life Rewards

Life rewards are the things that dogs love that you can use as incentives. Does your dog love to use his nose? Have him use this chance to smell as a reward. Is your dog going nuts for a car ride? Give him the reward of a ride! Does he love swimming? Train by the lake and let him swim for a reward. The rewards of life can be extremely strong. When your dog repeats his actions and you reward him with a life reward, it can be a powerful motivator for your dog to replicate his conduct. You usually don't use such incentives all the time or you wouldn't get a lot of training done, but if they're used once in a while, life incentives will make a huge impact on your dog.

Introducing the Clicker

Dogs do not immediately realize that the clicking sound of the clicker indicates that they did something you like. You've got to show them the meaning of the sound. You need to have a classic clicker condition that means a reward is coming.

This exercise tops the list of exercises you must teach your dog about the basics before you start training. You're going to use the clicker for all the drills, so show your dog that the clicking sound means a treat comes first.

1. Get five little, tasty treats. Just be close to your dog. When he's across the yard, you're not ready for this exercise, so make sure he's next to you. Don't ask your dog to lie down or do something else. This exercise is all about showing him that the sound of a click means a reward is coming, so you don't want to clutter it with something else.

2.Click on it once. Follow the click instantly with a treat. Do this five times.

3. Do this practice twice a day for the next two days.

Within a very short period of time, your dog's ears will perk up to the sound of a click. You will see his tail wagging. Now that the clicker is "powered up," it's time to start practicing!

Introducing a Target

Target is an incredibly valuable training technique for your dog's development. There are two main types of targets— nose targets and paw targets. You may teach a number of behaviors by encouraging your dog to raise his nose or paw to the mark. A nose target on your hand will turn into a Recall. Your dog will follow your hand to get on and off the furniture, and more. A paw target will teach your dog to go to his cottage or bed, or to sit outside the kitchen while you're preparing for dinner. Your first move will be to set goals for your dog.

Introducing a Nose Target

Your hand is the easiest nose target to start with. Below are the steps to demonstrate the nose target:

Target: The dog will touch his nose to your hand

What you're going to need: Clicker, treats.

1. Place the clicker in one hand. Keep the other hand, clean, with your palm facing your dog and your fingers down. Keep it 1 inch (2.5 cm) from the muzzle of your dog.

2. Many dogs will come forward to sniff or kiss your face. The second that your dog's nose is near your palm, press and pull your hand away. Give him a treat, please. Remove your hand so you won't touch him again until you're able to press and handle it again.

3. Repeat your palm, 1 inch (2.5 cm) in front of your dog's nose. Click, take your hand away, and pet him as he touches it.

Puppy Training For Beginners

4. Repeat for a total of 10 repetitions. Start the training session.

Tip: When your dog doesn't touch your side, you'll need to slowly shape your actions. If you raise your hand for the first time, at least your dog is likely to look at it. Click, remove your eye, and treat him for looking. Repeat a few times. The dog should start staring at the side more often than not. Keep clicking until he's looking at it regularly. Hold a minute to see if he nudges your hand. Be patient—let him think about it. Click and reward as he steps forward to touch your hand.

When your dog is continually scratching your hand, it's time to move your hand.

1. Place your palm 1 inch (2.5 cm) to the left of your dog's nose. Click and reward as he noses it. Do this by holding your palm 1 inch (2.5 cm) to the right of your dog's nose. Click and reward as he smells it.

2. Gradually start moving your hand further away from your dog, alternating between the left and the right. Click and treat each right answer when his nose touches your palm.

3. Now it's time for your dog to follow your side. Start with your hand close to the nose of your dog. When he goes to the nose, slowly

move it away from him in a straight line so that he follows it. Just go a few feet (about a meter) before you let him near it. Click it and treat it.

4. Gradually work until the dog follows the hand for more distances.

5. Repeat for a minimum of 10 repetitions. End the training session.

If your dog brushes your palm with his nose regularly, no matter when you place it, it's time to add the cue.

1. Just before you raise your hand, say the "Touch" cue in a polite voice. Click and reward when your dog touches your hand.

2. Repeat for a total of 10 repetitions. Start the training session.

Introducing a Paw Target

Choose an object that your dog should be able to reach with his paw. Bear in mind that some dogs are pleased with their paws, so your objective will be long-lasting. For instance, try a bottle of a coaster or a lid of a margarine tub. Here are the steps to teach a paw target:

Aim: Your puppy will touch his paw to a target.

Puppy Training For Beginners

It's time to add the cue, no matter when you present it.

What you're going to need: clicker, rewards, paw target.

1. Position the target near your dog on the ground. When your dog reaches out with a paw to strike the target, press, delete the target, and treat the target. However, this is not always the result. Most dogs are searching first with their noses. So, if your dog has a target, press, delete the target, and treat it. You're eliminating your target so you won't press it again until you're able to click and treat it again.

Why is it okay to press the target with his nose instead of pawing? Reason being that, for dogs, nosing and pawing are closely associated behaviors. When your dog starts with his nose, don't panic. He's going to turn to pawing soon.

2. When your dog has begun to paw the target, repeat about 10 times and then finish your training session.

3. If your dog has started nosing the target, repeat until the target is accurately nosed, about ten times. Present the target, then wait. Don't press the target for him. Just wait a minute. He'll soon get irritated when the nosing doesn't work anymore, so he'll try something else, probably a paw. The second time he hits the target with his paw,

tap, remove the target, and treat. Repeat 10 more times. Round up the training session.

Tip: Many dogs want to use their paws more than others, so they'll pick it up easily. Others may take a bit longer. Exercising a paw target may take one session, or a few sessions may be required. Only go as far as your dog can succeed. Some breeds, too, are more mouthy than others. You may notice that your sport-breed dog is trying to pick up the target. Should that be the case, just anchor the target with your foot so that he can't pick it up. This task is not a recovery. When you allow your dog pick up the target, it's going to be harder to teach him to paw it.

When your dog is constantly pawing, it's time to move the target.

1. Begin positioning the target at various locations, but within a few feet (about a meter) of your dog. Click and treat each time he hits the target with a paw.

2. Keep the target in the palm of your hand against the wall. Click and take care of every correct response.

3. Slowly start raising your target a little higher, but still at a safe height for your dog. Click and treat every correct response.

4. Repeat for a total of 10 repetitions. Finish the training session.

When your dog hits the target accurately with his paw, no matter where you pose it, it's time to add the cue.

1. Just before you raise your hand, say "Paw" once, in a polite voice. Click and treat when your dog paws the mark.

2. Repeat for a total of 10 repetitions. Close the training session.

PART II

PUPPY TRAINING

CHAPTER FIVE

EARLY TRAINING

Puppyhood is a beautiful, cute, messy, stressful, crucial time in a dog's life. You bring home your sweet little puppy, and you have all kinds of fantasies of how it will grow up. He's going to be a good family friend. He's going to be your best friend. He's going to love and protect your babies. He's going to do everything you ask him to do without protest or defiance. He's going to be an obedient or an agile star. He's going to be a therapy dog. He's never going to steal your socks, pee on the carpet, or growl at you. He's going to be fine!

Whether the dog meets those goals depends on the dog you brought home and, most importantly, on you and the people you communicate with.

The minute you meet him, you'll start bonding with your puppy. You should start teaching him as soon as you bring him home, which should be, at the youngest, about eight weeks of age. Puppies need to live with their mothers and littermates for around the first eight weeks to learn important social skills that will help them mature into stable, confident adult dogs. Be wary of any breeder who is allowing you to bring a puppy home sooner.

Young puppies are training sponges, but they have a very low attention span. This means that the training sessions will be very short, just a few minutes at a time. When you're raising your dog, you'll be doing much more than just teaching habits. When your hand offers treats, you're trying to show him that the hands that move toward him are healthy. It will help you with overall care, cleaning, and even pick up. You're also trying to show him that you're fun to be around and every training session will make your bond stronger. You will build a lot of productive relationships with your puppy and with training in general, which will build a strong base of trust between you and your puppy.

What You'll Need

There are a lot of items you can purchase for your puppy, so you may be tempted to go to the pet-supply shop to buy half the product! But here are the things that you will need specifically for your exercise.

Leash

Get a 4-to-6-foot (1-m) leash made from nylon, cotton, or leather. Don't go for a retractable leash. Retractable leashes are good for the exercise of your dog or for the training of certain advanced distance exercises, but are usually not suitable for walking or teaching your puppy. Even in a locked position, they don't offer you a lot of flexibility or control.

Plus, if you drop it and your puppy runs, the plastic handle would "chase" it and might scare it.

Be sure to find the size that's perfect for your puppy. For instance, if you have a toy-breed dog, you'll want a 1/4-inch (1.5-cm-thick) leash with a small clasp. Some leashes are short, but they still have thick clasps that could weigh down your little pup. Whether you have a big dog, a 3⁄4-inch-thick (2-cm-thick) or 1-inch-thick (2.5-cm-thick) leash is a safer option.

Collar

Choose a collar that's the perfect size for your puppy. You should always be able to get two fingers between your puppy's neck and his collar, keeping your fingers flat against his neck. Any bigger, and your puppy could catch his jaw or paw inside the collar, causing him to panic and injure himself. Both quick-snap or buckle collars are good options. Stop using choke pins, prongs, or electronic collars.

You will have to purchase an identification tag for the collar of your puppy. Pick one that won't bleach or leave a stain on his coat. Choose the perfect size for your puppy so that the tag doesn't dangle too far down his neck. Instead, if you want, you can get a collar engraved with your contact details instead of a sticker. Just make sure there's some form of marking on the collar. It should include the name of your dog and the best way to get in touch with you, such as your cell phone number.

Once your dog leaves the house, he will still wear an identification tag, even though you use a belt to attach your leash. You hope your puppy is never going to get away from you, but accidents are going to happen! If your dog ever gets lost or falls out of the door, the only chance he's got to find his way home is by marking.

Harness

Some dogs do better with harnesses. If you have a brachycephalic ('smoosh-faced') dog, such as a Pug, Japanese Bear, or Bulldog, then a harness is a better option for your dog than a collar and a leash for walking. Such breeds have breathing difficulties, particularly in hot weather or with strenuous exercise, so you don't want to obstruct their airways when they pull against a collar. And if you don't have a brachycephalic dog, the harness may be perfect for walking the dog.

There are a lot of harnesses on the market, but essentially they hold to a leash in two respects. Some of them have a leash loop on the back, near to the dog's shoulders. Others clip on the front of the dog's face.

Harnesses with a leash clip in the back are humane devices that you can use for your puppy. Bear in mind, however, that these types of harnesses are not going to help prevent your dog from pulling while walking on the leash. The collar is fixed to the back of the harness, which efficiently distributes the body weight of the dog.

A leash clip harness in the front will help discourage your puppy from pulling while walking on the leash by slowing down your puppy's forward motion. This form of harness can be a great tool for a puppy who likes to pull, particularly before you can teach him how to lead.

It's important to have the right fit for these harnesses. Incorrect fit may cause chafing under the front legs or chest. When the harness is rubbing on the puppy's chest position, he could get his paw or jaw stuck and panic, injuring himself. And if you want a front clip harness, make sure you follow the directions that come with it carefully or consult a professional who knows how to fit the harness properly.

When choosing a leash, try to find one that your dog can't get out of. Puppies can be wiggly! Although the harness is very easy to put on your puppy, bear in mind that it's just as easy for your puppy to get out of it and escape.

Head Halter

Whether you've got a very big dog, or if you're a little guy with a giant-breed dog, you may be interested in trying a head halter. It's also a nice tool for a dog who likes to climb on people. You should teach a puppy not to run, but a head halter can be a good training tool in the meantime.

The head halter is much more humane than the choke chain or prong collar, which exerts pressure on the trachea and needs yanking in order to "correct" the dog. A head halter literally monitors your puppy's brain. If a horse trainer can handle a big horse with a head halter, you can handle a puppy!

There are various head halters in the stores. No matter which model you pick, make sure it is properly fitted. Your dog will be able to relax and behave quickly. Make sure the loop of the nose does not chafe his muzzle or force it up towards his eyes so that he ends up squinting. Be sure to follow the instructions provided by the head halters or consult a professional with experience in fitting head stoppers properly.

Clicker

Clickers are available in most pet-supply stores and online. The most common form of clicker is a rectangular box. This type offers the loudest click, so if you're working with your dog in or out of class, the sound will travel nicely. There are also some models that have a softer press, which are perfect when you're practicing in a quiet place. These are also easier to press, which you may prefer if you have arthritis in your fingers or some other illness that makes it difficult to use your fingers. It's also helpful to buy a wrist coil to add a clicker to your package. This helps you to remove the clicker, but it's still connected to you. Some clickers have a loop that slides over your finger for convenience.

Once you start the clicker training, you will quickly discover that you and your dog enjoy it! So get a few clickers to keep handy all over the house.

Crate

Crates are important devices for the training of puppy. A crate is going to help you house-train your puppy and help keep him healthy from chewing unsuitable items. For house-training purposes, a crate should be big enough for a puppy to stand up, spread out, and move in. The goal is to confine the puppy enough to learn to maintain the bladder and the intestines. Some dogs are not going to ruin their "dens."

There are a variety of crates on the market. Choose a durable one that's going to endure dog chewing. Save the sweet canvas of travelers when your puppy is out of the chewing level. In general, a plastic or wire crate is a fine, strong option.

A standard plastic crate is a top and bottom that you bring together with nuts and bolts. You don't need any tools; you can move the bolts into place by hand. Puppies make messes, so it's very convenient to be able to take the top off the crate to clean the bottom. Some plastic crates are also approved for use by airlines. If you're interested in getting your puppy on an airplane, always consult with your particular airline in advance because they each have their own unique rules.

Wire crates come in a number of different types. Choose an epoxy coated wire to help avoid corrosion. You can get a crate that folds down "suitcase-style" and comes with a handle for quick handling and storage. Usually, a wire crate has a plastic tray in the bottom that can be removed for cleaning. If you choose a wire crate, be sure that the holes in the grate are not wide enough to allow your puppy to get a paw through. It could get stuck, and it could get hurt.

If you have a large-breed puppy, consider having a wire crate that contains a divider. The divider helps you to slowly increase the size of the room allocated to the puppy in the crate without having to buy new crates as the puppy grows.

You will find really cool designer boxes too. Some of them are made of rich woods and can also act as tables in the home. They are typically costlier than plastic or wire containers. If it comes to the training of a puppy, choose function over form. Spending a few hundred dollars on a designer crate that your puppy considers a chew toy is going to be a frustrating experience!

Toys

Toys are critical for the development of your puppy. Puppies love to chew, and the need to chew becomes stronger as they are teething. Giving your puppy suitable toys to chew on will give him a safe, reasonable alternative to chewing on items you do not want him to chew, such as your furniture or your shoes.

There are so many toys to choose from that it can be a little overwhelming. What makes the range of toys even more difficult to choose from is that different dogs prefer different toys. You're not going to know what your puppy likes until you try a few different toys.

There are some puppies that don't seem to like any toys, but you can teach your puppy to enjoy playing with toys instead of chewing off-limit objects.

Chew Toys

When choosing chew toys, purchase sturdy toys that are bigger than your puppy's muzzle. When your puppy gnaws a toy into bits that are tiny enough to fit fully into his mouth, you need to throw the toy away. This could easily be swallowed and squeezed, or it could get stuck in the digestive tract and require surgery to remove it.

The life span of a pet depends on the chewing style of your puppy. Some of the puppies are gentle with their toys and hold them into maturity. Others behave as if they will chew the tires! Choose toys that are suitable for the chewing style of your puppy. It's always best to err on the side of caution and pick a more robust toy if you're not sure about it. Some of the chew choices include deer or elk antlers, beef marrow bones, plastic toys, and rubber toys.

Interactive Toys

Interactive toys are perfect for keeping your puppies amused and centered. Fill a sturdy interactive device with the daily kibble of your puppy and some treats. As the dog works to remove the box, the box offers mental stimulation. Some toys are intended for long-lasting chew time, while others are more like dog puzzle games. Long-lasting ones are great for crate time or for occupying your puppy when you're unable to supervise him as closely as you need.

Tug toys are fun interactive toys too. Tug is a perfectly safe game for most puppies, but you'll find that when your puppy starts growing teeth, it may lose some of the teeth in the tug toy.

Balls

Balls are a special type of toy that will delight your puppy. Be sure to use a ball that isn't too small for your puppy's mouth. When you're using tennis balls, please make sure your puppy doesn't use it as a chew toy, as the rough coating could damage his enamel.

Flirt Pole

If you have a really energetic puppy, or maybe a herding type or a combination that likes to chase stuff, a flirting pole can be a fun toy that provides great exercise. A flirt pole is a long stick with a long cord attached to it. Normally there is a toy at the end of the string. It looks like a fishing rod except that you can't remove the rope normally. You will get the toy to bounce in various directions by flicking the pole to chase your puppy. It is a good toy for limited space too. When you have a designated area indoors where you can play with the flirt pole, it can be a perfect workout for your puppy on a rainy day when you can't take him outside to play.

Squeaky and Stuffed Toys

Other toys include those that make sounds and stuffed toys, and some are a mix of both. Some puppies are excited for squeaky toys. Also make sure your dog doesn't skip it and eat the squeaker or the stuffing. Stuffed animals should be specially made for dogs, not children's left over toys. So take note, if you have children in your life who have loved stuffed animals, giving your puppy a stuffed animal to chew on is only going to annoy him. He's not going to know the difference between his stuffed animal and your child's, and it won't be fair to yell at him or punish him for chewing on the wrong stuffed animal.

Puppy Games

You teach him what you want him to chew on by playing with your puppy with his toys. You're also teaching him to share his toys with you, rather than hoarding them to himself. Taking turns playing with his toys and then making him play with them on his own. You do want your puppy to know how to have fun. It's a good part of his growth not to become too reliant on you.

Having your puppy come to you should be easy at first, so get the most out of it! Crouch down, clap your hands, and make some kissing noises for your puppy. Praise him when he comes to you! Play with him, handle him— anything he finds rewarding. It should always be a good experience for your puppy to come to you. If you ever call him to punish him or yell at him, you're going to teach him to stay away from you. This is not the target.

You should play hide-and-seek with your dog too. At first, make it convenient. Lie around the corner and call your puppy to come and get you. Make a huge deal about it when he does! It is also going to create a good relationship with coming to you in your puppy's mind.

Good Exercise Makes a Healthy Dog

Puppies are full of energy for one minute, then suddenly napping in the next. When your puppy gets older, the naps are going to happen less and less. You might also wonder if there are batteries in your puppy because it never seems to slow down or rest!

Exercise can be an integral part of your puppy's health and growth and will also benefit you greatly during your training. If your dog doesn't get enough exercise, it'll show up in your training sessions. You can find that your puppy can't concentrate, is too excited, or totally ignores you. Although this is often an indication that your training session is too long, it is most frequently an indication that your puppy has not had enough exercise. Practicing with your puppy before training sessions will "take the pressure off" and help him better concentrate on learning.

How much exercise your puppy will require depends on his age and breed (or breed combination). Obviously, at eight weeks of age, puppies will require less exercise than at twenty-two weeks of age. A competitive breed such as the Weimaraner will require more exercise than a Maltese dog.

Think about what your dog was initially brought up to do— was it an aggressive activity? If so, the puppy will continue to exercise at the same amount, even though you chose not to perform the task. Your puppy's DNA is still optimized for the intended purpose of his breed. For instance, Dalmatians used to run in front of firehouse carriages, opening the way for horses to get through. It needed an athletic, energetic dog. If you don't want to run with your Dalmatian every day, you're going to have to find some way for him to spend that time.

Walking with you may be enough exercise for a young puppy, but once he reaches puberty, it's not going to be enough. You just don't walk quickly enough or long enough to get the heart rate up regularly for a decent workout. Plus, you usually want your puppy to walk happily by your side, which slows him down. That's why it's normal to hear people say that they're walking their dogs "miles (km) a day" and they still have the energy to burn.

It doesn't mean you're going to run marathons with your puppy. He's too young to do that. Do it safely as you exercise your puppy. The puppy's brain and heart may tell him to run around like a wild thing, but his body may not be ready. He's a puppy— not known for judgment! You are responsible for ensuring that the treatment of your puppy does not do more harm than good. Make sure you don't put too much pressure on your young puppy's body.

For those who are joggers, you don't begin by running a marathon on your first day. You prepare slowly. If you want to ride with your dog, you're going to have to train him slowly as well. He's not allowed to be your running buddy until he reaches physical maturity.

Discourage strenuous jumping before your puppy is fully grown because its growth plates are not yet closed and may cause harm if injured. For larger puppies, jumping on and off the furniture is typically fine (if you want to encourage it), but you shouldn't encourage them to practice jumping for agility until they're older. Small puppies can injure themselves by jumping off the couch.

Exercise and Weather

Weather can play a part in deciding if your puppy can exercise or play outdoors. Some puppies are going to be picky, so they don't want to go outside when it rains, but some dogs love to splash in puddles. Many dogs love to play in the snow, while others are sure they're going to be destroyed if they dare that. You'll need to know whether the temperature outside is too high for your puppy and take note of him when he's outside to make sure he's safe. If you're living in a really hot place, make sure your puppy doesn't overheat.

Signs of heat stroke in dogs includes:

- Excessive panting
- Drooling, with thick, sticky saliva
- Bright red tongue
- Vomiting
- Diarrhea
- Dizziness

If your dog has these symptoms, immediately remove him from the heat and call your veterinarian or emergency clinic.

Another heat-related threat is your puppy's paws. Puppies don't wear shoes, but walking on hot asphalt will burn your puppy's paw pads. Whether your area has sidewalks or grass to walk on, it's going to help in the heat, but some areas don't have sidewalks, and people have to walk their dogs in the street. The asphalt is going to get really dry. If your puppy starts jumping on the ground and acting as if he's in pain then check his paws. He may be getting heat blisters.

Conversely, if you're living in an area that's getting very cold, you also need to be careful with outdoor activities. Did you know that dogs can get hypothermia and even frostbite? Toy breeds, dogs with thin coats, and puppies are especially vulnerable to hypothermia, which means that the body temperature drops too much.

Signs of hypothermia:

- Lethargy
- Violent shivering
- Weak heartbeat
- Coma

If you think your puppy has hypothermia, wrap him in a blanket and put him inside where it's dry. Call your veterinarian or emergency clinic right away.

Frostbite, in which part of the body freezes, is usually followed by hypothermia. Popular target areas are ears, ear tips, and paw pads. If your puppy has frostbite, the fur may be pale white or blue in the affected regions. As the circulation returns to the region, the skin may appear bright red and may start to peel. Hours later, it will turn dark. The places are going to be very painful. When you think your dog has frostbite, apply warm— not hot— water to the affected areas and call your veterinarian or emergency clinic.

The Secret to Good Puppy Training

You play the most important part in the training and future of your puppy. This is a lot of responsibility! Be patient— with your puppy as well as yourself. Training is hard work, and you are bound to make a few mistakes along the way, particularly if this kind of canine training is new to you. Yet, you can do that. Your puppy will test your patience from time to time, but remember that he's just a puppy. You need to show him what you want, in words he can understand.

Don't use rough tones for your puppy when you're practicing. When you were in school, if your teacher gave you all her orders with a rough tone, it would have been pretty stressful. You don't have to scream at your dog to teach him to do what you want. Keep a better tone of voice when he's doing something awful. (Better still, tell him not to do anything like that.)

Use a friendly voice to interact with and train your puppy. In particular, you don't want to use his name or the Recall cue in a derogatory way, such as "FIDO! Come over here!" If you're upset with your dog, it's just going to encourage him to avoid you when you call his name or tell him to come to you. This isn't what you want him to know!

Set guidelines on what you're going to allow and what you're not going to allow, and make sure your family sticks to the same rules. For instance, if you don't want a dog to sleep on your bed, don't let your new puppy sleep on the bed just because he's a little tired in his first few days in a new home. It's going to be too frustrating and upsetting for your dog to get used to sleeping with you on the bed just to get booted when he gets bigger.

If you don't want your grown dog to leap on you, don't encourage your puppy to leap up on you. It's very tempting to make your cute little puppy hop up to kiss your cheek, but that's rewarding his jumping actions. If you continue to reward this conduct, it's going to become a pattern that's going to be harder to correct. It's frustrating to your dog if you let him jump for a while and then you don't want him to jump on you again.

It's best to start with limitations and reduce them as your puppy goes through training so that he can gain control and obey your cues. For instance, if you don't mind a dog jumping on you, that's all right. But you might have other people in your life, such as elderly people or young children, that may be hurt by a dog jumping on them. Teach your puppy not to jump on people right from the start when you carry him home. As he gets older and you train him to respond to your cues, you can teach him the cue to jump up. You can only tell him to stand up when he gets his cue. This should make it easier to control who he does and doesn't jump on.

It's the same as encouraging a dog to get on the furniture. Maybe you don't mind if your grown dog is snuggling with you on the sofa, but a puppy may throw himself at you when you're on the sofa having a snack, and might make a mess or even injure you. Teach your puppy not to get on the furniture right from the start. As he gets older and you educate him, you can show him a sign that he's allowed to get on the furniture. This means that you'll be able to tell when he gets up on the sofa.

CHAPTER SIX

HOUSE-TRAINING

House-training can be very stressful for the owners of puppies. It's never fun to clean up the mess. There may be moments when you think your puppy is purposely peeing in the house just to annoy you, but that's never the case. Puppies are not peeing or pooping out of spite. Defecation is a normal biological event. The dog probably doesn't realize why you don't want him to pee on the floor. Even if you think you've been really specific on where you want him to be replaced, that might not be the case.

House-training requires discipline, flexibility, and direct communication. This often requires you to keep an eagle-eyed watch on your puppy. The expression "monitoring your puppy" really means that you need to be like an FBI Witness Protection Team, watching your puppy every minute to avoid accidents. Puppies can pee really quickly! You can turn your back for just a few minutes, and when you turn back around you discover a fresh puddle on the floor.

Your puppy can only eliminate in the wrong places if you let him go. Either he has too much independence or he doesn't have enough control, or you haven't taken him to his exclusion spot often enough. Each time he excretes in the wrong place, he's in the wrong. Your goal is to treat your puppy in such a way that he has very little chance of excreting where you don't want him to and every opportunity to excrete where you want.

Your first house-training choice is where you want your puppy to excrete: indoors or outdoors? Select either of them, please. When you want your puppy to excrete indoors sometimes, but outdoors at other times, it's just too hard for your puppy. Keep it easy, please.

Outdoor defecation means that your dog is not going to pee or poop inside the house. Indoor defecation ensures that the dog will be excrete on pee pads or in a litter box. So, for instance, if you want to teach your puppy on how to excrete outside, you wouldn't put pee pads inside the house and allow him to eliminate there.

When you know where you want your puppy to eliminate, it's time to start containment training. A crate is the perfect device for this.

Crate Training

A crate is a shelter for your dog that you can use to make house-training much easier. Used correctly, it will help encourage your puppy to keep his bowels and bladder trained because most puppies don't want to litter their dens. In addition to house-training, there are also advantages of crate-training for puppies.

- Crates keep your puppy away from eating or swallowing anything that might harm him, such as electrical wires or small objects that he might swallow.
- Crates protect your puppy from chewing destructively on things you'd like him to leave alone, such as your furniture, clothes, children's toys, carpets, and more, which, in effect, stops you from becoming mad at your puppy for excessive chewing!
- Crates help show the dog how to be on its own. You can't be with your dog all the time, so it's good for him to know how to be on his own and be fine with it.
- Crates help keep a puppy alive while recovering from sickness, injury, or surgery. For instance, whether your puppy gets spayed or neutered, it's going to have to rest some time later. When the anesthesia is gone, your puppy is likely going

to be able to zip around long before he should! A crate is going to keep him from having too much action. Also, puppies will often zig when they should zag and can end up pulling a muscle or causing a soft tissue injury. Your veterinarian can prescribe a few days or weeks of crate rest. How do you maintain a wiggly puppy? The answer is you use a crate.

- The prices are excellent for flying. If your car is large enough to accommodate your puppy's crate, it will ride in the crate for safety purposes. Dogs will never be left in your car while driving. If you were in a car crash, the dog will be a projectile. (If your vehicle isn't big enough for a crate, you should get a canine safety belt.) When you take your puppy on a ride, the crate will be a comfortable den to give him some protection to prevent him from getting into trouble. It's going to be humiliating if your puppy pees all over your grandma's fancy rug, so get your puppy's crate on the plane.
- •Crates are more productive for house-training than simply placing your puppy in a room, such as a kitchen, a laundry room, or a bathroom. If your puppy has a lot of space, he can pee or poop in the corner and just walk over to a clean spot. He will not learn to keep his bladder and bowels under control in a room as easily as he will in a crate of the right size. Plus,

some puppies are known to chew through wooden doors or leap over baby gates to escape from rooms.

Introduced correctly, a crate can be a safe haven for your puppy. He's going to have a cozy place to take breaks when he's depressed or tired. You may notice that he's ready to go to his nap crate. To do so, you need to crate-train your puppy to learn to love his new home.

Crate Location

Where do you place the crib of your puppy? Preferably, place it in an area where you normally hang out, such as a dining room or a living room. It's all right if you want to push the crate into your bedroom at night. In fact, it might help your puppy adjust to your home quicker, as it may feel better to be near you.

Don't try to get the crate off in a room by itself, such as in a laundry room or another room where you don't spend a lot of time. The dog needs to be part of your family, and if you want him to be close to you, you need to keep his crate close by. He's not going to be in the crate all the time, but when he's very young, he's going to spend a lot of time in his crate when you can't keep a close eye on him — so you'll want him nearby.

Crate Accessories

Puppies are supposed to have access to water in their cages. Stop using plastic bowls that your dog can chew on. You can get stainless steel bowls or "coop cups" that are connected to the crate handle. When you notice that your dog constantly splashes his water and makes a mess, you will not be able to contain the water in his crate. In this situation, make sure he has a lot of exposure to water while he's out of his crate.

You might try placing a crate pad or a blanket in the crate, but don't be surprised if your puppy chews it. Puppies are in love with chewing. If your dog doesn't chew a pillow, it's all right to leave it in the cage. Yet if you see any sign of chewing, get the blanket out of the crate. If he were to break up pieces and eat them, they could get trapped in his intestines, requiring surgical removal. The dog is going to be perfect in a cage without a blanket or a pillow. When he grows up a bit and gets out of his chewing phase, you can try putting one in there again.

You may also find an elegant crate cover made of fabric to drape over your puppy's crate for some protection and a more comfortable setting. Crate covers work for some dogs, while some may find a way to take the cloth out of the crate and chew on it. If your dog is a chewer, leave the crate uncovered.

Don't put pee pads in the cage of your puppy. You may think it's a good idea to put them down to absorb urine in case they pee, but that's not a good idea. Many pee pads are equipped with a fragrance that encourages puppies to excrete, which could tell your puppy to excrete in his crate. And if the pads are not scented, if your dog pees on them and the urine is absorbed, it's going to show him that it's okay to excrete in the crate. Crate training is intended to help teach your dog to keep his bladder under control, not to eliminate in his den. If you want to use pee pads to encourage your puppy to eliminate indoors, that's fine — just don't put them in your puppy's crate.

Introduction of the Crate

The crate will also be a fun experience for your puppy. Never use the crate for reprimanding. Here are the steps you should take to bring your puppy to the crate. Bear in mind that not all of these steps will happen in one session. Keep the sessions short— just a few minutes at a time— with breaks in between.

Goal: The puppy should learn to go to his crate and stay there.

What you're going to need: clicker, rewards, crate.

1. Take your puppy to the location where you set up the crate. Click and treat for some interest in the crate, even though he's just staring

Puppy Training For Beginners

at it. Don't tempt him to the crate with the treats. It's going to be safer if he tries it on his own and then gets a reward treat. Some puppies are so dependent on food that they could go back into the crate for more, but then they're too upset to figure out where they are that they're just not paying attention. Use the treats as bonuses, not bribes.

2. Your puppy is expected to start going towards the crate or even sniffing it. Press and handle for any interactions.

3. Gradually work when the dog places one paw inside the crate. Click it and treat it.

4. As long as your puppy puts one foot in the crate securely, wait and press. He's supposed to try something new, like placing two paws inside the crate, to get a reward. Click it and treat it!

5. Work where your puppy is going all the way to the crate. Select and treat all the right answers.

Now that your puppy is happily going to his bed, it's time to add the cue.

1. Just before your puppy comes to the crate, send the sign "Kennel up!" and go to the kennel, or "Crate up!" with a polite tone. Click and treat as he goes in.

2. It's time to shut the door. Cue "Kennel up," let your puppy get into the crate, shut the crate door, and then click and give him a treat through the crack. Immediately open the door, and if he wants, let him come out. When he wants to sit in the cage, give him a few more treats.

3. When your puppy reaches his crate and you can shut the door for a second, slowly increase the amount of time you hold the door closed. Cue "Kennel up," let your puppy get into the crate, shut the door, wait a few seconds, and then click and move a treat through the crate door. If he's still quiet, wait a few seconds and then give him another treat through the crate door. Open the door, and if he wants, let him go. Repeat a few times.

4. Gradually increase the amount of time you leave your puppy in crate with the door closed. Only let him out if he's quiet. When he starts pawing or crying or barking at the crate door, don't let him go. Keep waiting for him to calm down and be quiet before you let him go. During the next replay, reduce the time so that your puppy can be effective.

Up until now, you've been living with your puppy near his crib. It's time to teach him to enjoy his crate without you in the vicinity.

1. Cue "Kennel up," let your puppy get into the crate, shut the door, click and treat. Move into the door and step straight out. Give another treat through the crate door and then open the door and let your puppy out if he wants (as long as he's still). Repeat a few times.

2. Gradually work so you can leave the room for longer periods of time. Return a few times and feed your puppy with a treat through the crate door, as long as your puppy stays quiet.

3. If you're five minutes away, start leaving your puppy with a food-stuffed rubber toy or a chew bone to enjoy when you're home. This is going to make his time in the crate more satisfying.

Tip: Don't let your dog get out of his crate when he screams, whines, or barks. You're just trying to show him that screaming, moaning, or barking means you're going to let him out. Just wait for him. When you don't, you'll regret it later, because it's going to be harder to convince him to sit in his crate. Your puppy will need protection for some time, so be careful with your training now. Continue making the crate fun, perform in a short time, and he'll soon grow to enjoy his crate.

This training may take several sessions over a few days, but you're going to have to crate your puppy overnight on the first night you've got him home. And what are you going to do if you haven't done your crate training yet? Okay. Just put your puppy in his crate, give him a couple of treats and a toy, and leave him there overnight. For the first few nights that you crate your puppy, if you haven't finished your training, and if he's never been conditioned by his previous home, he will protest. Check it out. Is he fed up with anything? Is he really hurt? If not, don't let him get out of the crate. Often it helps, if the crate is in your bedroom, to place your fingers through the crate door so that he can smell them and feel comforted that you're nearby. But don't let him go if he's going to cause a fight. Be bold, calm your puppy down! When you finish your crate-training, he's going to enjoy his bed, and you're going to be able to enjoy your sleep.

Know, if you have a very young (about eight weeks old) puppy, he may not be able to go all night without a potty break. In this situation, just take him out for a potty break and carry him back to his crate immediately with a treat. You can also give him a treat during the early days of crate-training when he goes to his crate to help develop a good relationship with it.

If you're home with your dog, you can keep him out of the cage as much as you want, as long as you can supervise him properly. Make sure you crate him regularly when you're at home, though, so he doesn't necessarily equate your departure with crate time. You might, for instance, crate him with a food-stuffed rubber toy when you're cooking and eating dinner.

Setting Schedules

Determine the puppy's eating schedule and potty schedule. In general, it is not recommended to free-feed a puppy. If he's eating all day, he's going to have to excrete all day, making it harder to house-train him.

Puppies under the age of six months are supposed to eat three meals a day. Only set the food down for about 15 minutes. At 15 minutes, remove the food bowl, even if there food is left. When you feed your puppy on a daily basis, he'll soon know when it's time to eat. Maybe he'll end up reminding you!

Attempt to arrange the feeds equally. You don't want to make the last feed too late in the evening because then your puppy will have to excrete in the middle of the night. It's also safe to take your puppy's water about an hour before bedtime to help and his need to pee during the night. Only make sure that he had plenty of opportunities to drink water provided during the day.

If your routine is different on the weekends, your puppy's routine will not be the same. Puppies do their best and grow better with consistency, so keep their feeding schedule as near the same times as possible every day of the week.

Your puppy's potty schedule can depend heavily on the age of your puppy and, to a certain degree, the breed or breed combination. Very young puppies (approximately 8 to 16 weeks of age) may require more frequent potty breaks than six-month-old puppies. Toys and small dogs also tend to require more frequent potty breaks.

In general, puppies need to eliminate when they wake up (even from their naps), when they sleep, when they play, and when they bathe. You're going to be pretty busy having to take your puppy on a potty break at these times as well as every few hours. As your puppy gets older, he's going to need less frequent potty breaks.

If you regularly take your puppy to his defecation spot, and he doesn't excrete, then start reducing the amount of potty breaks you're giving him. There are eight potty breaks every day, according to the sample schedule illustrated here. The typical adult dog wants about four potty breaks a day. And, as your puppy ages, you're slowly going from around eight potty breaks a day to four. Each puppy is an individual and may need more or less potty breaks. When your dog ages into a senior citizen, he will need more potty breaks again.

Schedules help you remain organized and help you practice more effectively, but puppies don't always know your schedules! And know the signs that your puppy shows when he needs to potty. Remember that very young puppies cannot give you a lot of notice at all. They have very little power, and they have not yet learned to understand the feeling that tells them that they have to eliminate. When your dog gets older, he's going to send you more signs. He may whine. He might start sniffing the ground or moving in circles. If you see these signs, you can play it safely and take it to the elimination spot.

Training Your Puppy to Potty Outside

When you don't have a yard for your puppy to excrete in, but you want him to excrete outside, you'll need to teach him how to excrete while walking outside. Or maybe you've got a yard, but ultimately you want to go on a trip with your dog and teach him how to avoid eliminating on various surfaces (also called "substrates"), such as grass, pine straw, rocky areas, and the like. Some dogs can develop special preferences if they have not been trained to avoid them in different environments. For instance, if your puppy only excretes on grass and you travel to a location with mostly rocky terrain, your dog can "keep" it for hours rather than go to an unfamiliar surface. So save yourself the next hours of inducement under the burden of travel.

Teach your puppy that various places outside are appropriate for defecation.

Just sending your dog out on a potty schedule isn't going to motivate him to eliminate outdoors. Puppies are quickly disturbed by this. Your puppy doesn't know you want him to excrete outside. He may assume you took him outside to check out the neighbors or find bugs. You need to keep him focused on the job you want him to do. You should also take your puppy out on the leash to do this.

When you're attached to your dog, you can restrict the amount of environmental damage you're experiencing. The fenced yard is not enough to keep distractions to a minimum for the average puppy. As you hold the leash, you can gently guide him to the area where you want him to excrete, whether in your yard or on the sidewalk as you walk, and keep him from running off to explore. Leashing your puppy will help make potty breaks more effective, as you're not going to chase your puppy all over the yard as he gets distracted by every smell and sight.

He can learn to eliminate easily, which is incredibly helpful if you have a busy schedule, travel, or need to track his defecation for health purposes.

Leashing your puppy will also help you motivate your puppy to eliminate in bad weather. Yeah, that means you've got to go outside too! In order to successfully train your puppy in the home, you've got to go out with him. You've got to be there at the second he's trying to defecate so you can reward him. When your dog is completely house-trained, you won't still have to go outside with him.

Goal: Your puppy is going to defecate outside.

What you're going to need: medications, plastic cleaning bags, collar.

1. Hide the treats from your dog. Some dogs are going to be so focused on rewards that they might be too busy to defecate.

2. Leash the dog. Take him out to his elimination spot. If you want to train your puppy to defecate while walking, don't walk too far before finding an elimination spot. You're going to know where your puppy's going to defecate. If you always pick a spot early on your stroll, it will develop the habit of first eliminating and then enjoying the rest of the stroll. If you want a spot near your house, you can also go back and dispose of the poop bag so that you don't have to carry it all along the way.

3. As soon as he wants to defecate, say "Go potty" in a friendly voice. If you're out for ten minutes and your puppy doesn't defecate, bring him back inside and watch him closely for about 15 minutes, and then repeat the process.

4. As soon as your dog is done defecating, thank him and give him a treat.

5. Play or walk away with your puppy for a few minutes. You should let him go if you want (as long as you have a fenced yard). You don't want to take him inside immediately, or you might tell him that removal means the time outside is over.

Repeat Steps 1–5 for every potty break.

Tip: Keep in mind that this is a process. Your dog won't be able to predict that he needs to excrete until he's at least four months old. If your puppy goes without any incidents for a week, don't be fooled into thinking he's fully trained. Any incident he has inside is going to set you back a little. So be careful, handle your puppy, and adopt the training program. Keep up with the plan until you have months, not days, of progress.

When your dog goes out on a normal leash with you and defecates with the use of a cue, it's time to start weaning off the leash if you

Puppy Training For Beginners

prefer. These steps presume that you have a properly fenced yard that you want your puppy to defecate within. Your dog will never be allowed to leave the leash in an unfenced yard or on a stroll. These steps will encourage you to send your puppy out to the yard to excrete while you stay by the door.

1. Take your puppy out to go potty while following the previously established house-training plan, but let the puppy drag the leash this time. Monitor him very closely. Make sure the rope doesn't get tangled with something. When he's trying to excrete, thank and treat. Continue until he defecates without stressing you.

2. Take your dog out to defecate while following the house-training program, except this time without a leash. Monitor him very closely. When he's trying to excrete, thank and treat. When your dog manages to excrete easily without being on the lead, move on to Step 3. When he wants to run around and play, go back and keep the leash for a week and then try Step 1.

3. Take your puppy out and get rid of the house-training system, but slowly stay away from your puppy. Always thank him when he defecates, and when he comes back to you, give him a treat. If at any point your puppy gets too distracted, reduce the distance between you and the puppy then gradually work back up to more distance. (Some

puppies will have a habit of eliminating quickly by this point, but some will still be easily distracted. All reactions are natural. Just go at your puppy's pace.) Your aim is to get to the point that you can sit by the door while you're taking your puppy out to the yard to defecate.

Tips: Please don't be discouraged if things go well for a bit and then you experience a setback. The outside has a lot of smells and distractions for your puppy more so than the inside of your house. You can have a few weeks of success, and then one day, your teenage puppy goes out and gets obsessed with one corner of the yard, totally ignoring your warning to eliminate. It may be that a rabbit recently paid a visit to your yard, or a neighborhood cat used your yard as an elimination spot. Note, puppies and young dogs have a short attention span. So, if you have a stressful house-training experience, that's normal. Only stick with the plan, be patient, and wait for your puppy's lack of attention. If possible, go back a few steps to the point where your puppy is good so that you can stay on track. You don't want to make a momentary distraction a daily habit for your puppy.

Training Your Puppy to Excrete While Indoors

Training your puppy to excrete indoors can be handy whether you stay in a high-rise apartment or have a small or medium dog. Puppies usually have to eliminate as soon as they wake up, and pushing a puppy down fifteen flights to get outside is troublesome. Some people can't make it home for a midday break, or they live in an environment that isn't conducive to an outdoor elimination. This is when litterbox or paper preparation can be very convenient.

Indoor removal can be both convenient and uncomfortable for travel. When you're in a hotel room, it would be easy to set up a defecation area for your dog so you won't have to think about getting him outside. Nevertheless, if you take him to visit friends or family, they will not accept or encourage you to have an indoor elimination station.

To begin with, pick if you want to train your puppy to defecate in a litter box or on paper or pee pads. Litterboxes come in a variety of different types. Some need paper, others use sod or artificial turf. Remember that dog litter is different from cat litter! Don't put kitty litter in your puppy's litter box; it might not be safe for him. Sod or turf is a safe option if you decide to train your puppy to potty outside as well.

Goal: The puppy must discharge indoors at a particular spot.

What you're going to need: elimination station, treatments.

1. Hide your dog's treats. Some puppies are going to be so focused on rewards that they may be too busy to defecate.

2. Bring your puppy to the elimination spot. As soon as he begins to excrete, give your cue (like "Go potty") in a friendly voice. As soon so your dog is done, thank him and treat him.

3. If you wait ten minutes and your puppy doesn't defecate, confine him or closely track him for about 15 minutes, and then try step 2 again.

Repeat Steps 1–3 for each potty break.

When your dog is eliminating on a regular basis, it's time to start training him to move on to the elimination spot on his own, without you having to go with him.

1. Bring your puppy to the elimination site, but stop about a step away from the spot. Let your puppy go on the rest of the way by himself. Employ the house-training plan outlined above. Don't forget to praise him and treat him when he defecates. When your puppy continues to the elimination spot on a regular basis, you're ready for the next step.

2. Slowly step away from the elimination spot, one step at a time, each time your puppy defecates. Employ the home-training program.

Your goal is to finally be able to send your puppy out of another room to his elimination spot.

Tips: When your puppy misses a litterbox or a pee pad at any moment, go back to the last point where it was successful. Stay at that step for a week, and then try to push further forward.

Through patience and practice, the puppy will start going to the elimination place on its own when he has to excrete. It's going to take some time before he's stable, so he must be mature enough to recognize the feeling that indicates he's going to defecate. Keep track of your puppy. If you notice he messes outside the elimination spot, check first to make sure that the path to the elimination spot is not blocked. For instance, if there's a spot in your bathroom, was anyone in there with a door shut? Or was there something potentially scary, like a parked vacuum cleaner, in the puppy's way? If you can't find anything that hinders the road to the elimination position, back up in your preparation. Go back to watching your puppy more closely for a few weeks, and then slowly step away again. Don't be distracted by that! Occasionally, it is very normal to have house-training incidents. Only stick to the plan faithfully and be patient.

Future Training

Once your puppy knows that you want him to relieve himself in a certain place, you can do some advanced training if you want.

Dog Doors

Some people assume that if they have a dog door, their puppy will immediately learn how to excrete outside the building. It's true that some puppies are innately wired to excrete out of doors, but not all puppies are, and you shouldn't rely on the door to do your home-training work for you. Plus, should you ever move to a place that doesn't have a dog door for your puppy, it might get confused.

Another downside of using dog doors with unattended puppies is that your puppy may carry stuff from outside to the inside that you might not appreciate! Dogs have been known to carry objects indoor ranging from sticks to live animals. Puppies are naturally curious, and the likelihood of your puppy bringing something to your home is high. He could take your nice stuff outside, too, and leave them there.

If you bring a new puppy home and you already have another older dog or dogs in your home that use a dog door on a regular basis, don't depend entirely on them to train your puppy at home. For instance, puppies often learn to follow other dogs outside to eliminate. So, as the other dogs pass away and are no longer around to lead them, they may decide to eliminate in the house. Make sure you're the one who shows your puppy what you want.

When your puppy has been doing well in his house-training for a couple of months, it should be safe to bring him to the dog door.

Goal: The puppy is going through the door of a house.

What you're going to need: clicker and reward.

1. Sit by the door of your house with your puppy. Press on some interest in the dog door, even if he's just staring at it.

2. After a few clicks to demonstrate interest, your puppy will start running towards or nosing the dog door. Click it and treat it. Gradually operate where your puppy opens the door with his nose. Click it and treat it.

3. When your puppy is puzzled or a little unsure about the door, open it yourself and leave it open. Don't let it slam closed or it may startle him. Click and treat each exploratory action.

4. Gradually navigate where your puppy is going through the dog door. Click and treat any right answer.

5. Go outside the door with the dog and repeat the move. Just because your puppy tries to get through the door one way doesn't mean he's going to realize that he can get back in!

Tip: This can take one or more sessions, depending on your puppy. Several times, puppies may aggressively charge straight through the door, while others may be more reluctant. Every reaction is natural, so just go as fast as your puppy is comfortable with and you will succeed.

Teaching Your Puppy to Ring a Bell

As your house-training progresses, you should teach your puppy to send you a warning that he needs to relieve himself. This action is for a puppy who is conditioned only to eliminate outdoors.

Goal: The puppy is going to ring a bell to go outside.

What you're going to need: Bell attached to a long cord, also attached to the door leading out, clicker, rewards, leash. To decide the length of the rope to be used, position the bell so that it does not hang higher than the shoulder of your puppy. You want your puppy to be able to paw the bell quickly. Attach the bell to the door you're using to carry your dog in and out for elimination. You can only use this door for training purposes.

Puppy Training For Beginners

1. Sit next to the doorbell. Click and treat your puppy if he shows any fondness in the bell for some purpose, even though he's just staring at it. Then he's expected to start showing increased interest and begin to nose the bell. Click it and treat it. Instead, if you've already taught him his target cue, you can guide him to the "Touch" button. Select and handle all the right answers.

2. If your puppy rings the bell on a daily basis, it's time to tell your puppy that ringing the bell means you're going to open the door and take it outside. You're going to need to leash him for this process. If it's time for a potty break, let your puppy lie down and wait at the door. Just be still and wait for the bell to sound. Tap, feed, and then open the door to carry him outside. Give him his signal to eliminate, and then give him a reward for doing so. Repeat for every potty break.

3. Through practice, your puppy will know that when the bell rings, you will open the door. You're not going to be by the door one day, but you're going to hear the bell ring. You remember, this is your puppy playing! Drop what you're doing right away, go to your puppy, leash it, and open the door. At this point, you don't need to click anymore because he's mastered the habit of ringing the bell.

4. Give him ten minutes to eliminate. If he does, show him attention and treat him. If he doesn't, just carry him back inside. The

dog still hasn't realized at this point that ringing the bell is just for when he needs to defecate. He's discovered that ringing the bell means he's going outside. By leaching your puppy, you'll quickly decide whether he really needs to go potty or just wants to play, so you can easily bring him in if he feels it's playtime.

5. Repeat Steps 3 and 4 every time you hear the bell ring from your puppy. You might find that your puppy rings a lot at first! It's usual.

Tip: If you think that your puppy really wants to go outside and play, so you don't open the door, you're going to tell him that bell ringing doesn't mean anything. It is going to put the preparation off. You may also notice that he's defecating indoors because you haven't let him out. So even if you think your puppy is playing, go and open the door. So long as you tether him so he can't run and play around, you'll soon tell him that ringing a bell is only for when he wants to eliminate.

Cleaning Up Messes

Even with the best intentions, there are bound to be moments when your dog excretes where you don't want him to do — this is normal. Your goal in house-training should be to reduce the number of times this occurs, but don't overreact when it does.

If you catch your puppy in the act of defecating, try use the 'No' sternly looking! And then take him to his restroom (leave him if you train him outside to defecate). When he's done in his elimination place, applaud him. You need to make it clear that you're not pleased when he defecates in an inappropriate place, but you love it when he excretes in the designated location.

You don't have to use harsh discipline, or you might cause major problems. Just use your authoritative speech. Never use your hands to mock your puppy, and never roll up a newspaper to hit your puppy. This is not going to help him to stop defecating in the house at all. Instead, it's either going to teach him to be scared of you, or to hide from you when next he wants to defecate. That is how you make a puppy that hides in closets or under tables while excreting. That's not what you're trying to say to him!

If you didn't catch your puppy defecating, you can't threaten him. He's forgotten what you're ranting about. Only be more diligent with your monitoring to keep this from happening again.

CHAPTER SEVEN

BASIC ETIQUETTE AND LIFE SKILLS

As a puppy owner, you have a responsibility to ensure that your puppy behaves properly when it's out in public. Puppies are babies, so they don't understand the way adults do. You're going to teach your puppy manners, but in the meantime, you're going to have to control his actions to keep him from being a nuisance or unintentionally harming you or another animal.

Big Expectations

There are also assumptions in general for canine good manners. Well-mannered dogs and puppies:

- Are leashed in public wherever possible. They're not playing wild in the neighborhoods. Puppies that run loose can easily get hurt by cars, unfriendly loose dogs, or even people who don't like weird dogs coming into their yards.

- It is not allowed to run to another dog without the permission of the owner of that dog. Although it's nice if your puppy is social, invading another dog's space without permission is rude. Puppies frequently greet with excitement, which is not always welcomed by other dogs. It could make your puppy get a little upset if he gets in the face of a dog that doesn't like his greeting.

- Are not supposed to climb on people. A jumping puppy is normally cool! But that doesn't mean that everyone loves a puppy jumping on them. And depending on the size of your dog, someone may have been inadvertently injured.

- Do have their waste cleaned up by the responsible owners. When your dog excretes on other people's belongings, you should pick it up and dispose of it. It's just part of being the owner of a puppy.

You can do most of the tricks just by leaching your dog when you're out in public or when you've brought guests over. You will stop him from getting into the most trouble that way. When you teach him, you're not going to have to handle him too closely.

Safety Net: The Collar and Leash of Your Dog

Puppies are not born to like their collars or being directed by their leashes. It's normal for a puppy to scratch his back, attempt to disengage from a leash, or put the brakes on, and refuse to move when first leached. You're going to have to teach your dog to enjoy his collar and his leash. He'll soon learn that they're synonymous with walking, playing, and having fun.

Goal: The puppy should learn to wear a collar (or a harness).

What you're going to need: jewelry, candy, toys.

1. Allow your puppy to sniff the necklace. Give him a treat, please. Say it.

2. Put your leash on your puppy. Only give him three treats in a row. Remove the tie, but only if he's not pawing it. Repeat a few times.

3. Put your collar on your puppy. Give him a couple of treats. Let him wear it for a few seconds then remove it. Don't remove it if he paws it. Repeat as much as you can.

Puppy Training For Beginners

4. Put your necklace on your puppy. Offer him a treat, then play with him. Engage him with his toys, show him a lot of attention, and tell him how cute he is. For a few minutes, remove the collar and remain silent, removing your attention. Repeat, make a huge noise about him when he's wearing a collar, and be silent when you take it off.

Tips: When your dog wraps around his collar or squeals with it, do not take it off. Instead, distract him with a toy. If you remove it while he's pawing it, you're going to show him that his action is going to try to get you to take off the leash. Just make sure that the collar fits correctly so that he can't get his jaw or paw inside. Remember to check it out regularly, as puppies grow fast. A collar that suits perfectly one day could be too tight the next.

When you get your puppy used to wearing a collar, it's time for the leash to be attached. These are the measures.

Goal: The puppy must learn to wear a leash attached to his collar (or harness).

What you're going to need: leash, collar, treats.

1. Have the medications ready. Put the collar on your puppy and add the leash to it. Give three treats to your dog.

2. Let your dog pull the rope to a secure place where it won't get tangled. Supervise him closely to ensure he's healthy. Offer your dog treats randomly as long as he doesn't chew on his leash.

3. Gently take the rope and keep it. Give your dog a couple of treats.

4. Continue walking and inspire your dog to come along with you. If he's putting the brakes on, don't say something. Just wait for him. Only apply enough pressure to tighten the cord slightly; don't yank it. If he starts walking with you, give him a lot of attention and a couple of treats.

5. Repeat until your dog allows you to tether it quickly. Use gentle pressure only if necessary. Don't use the leash to yank your puppy to you.

6. Teaching Self Control:

Slow Down

There are moments when you just want your puppy to be quiet and cool, to settle down. This may be a really tough thing for a dog to do!

Goal: The puppy is going to settle down and be happy.

What you're going to need: clicker, treats.

1. Leap, brush his back, use a high-pitched voice, or run around to get your puppy really excited. After he's all riled up for a couple of seconds, stand still. Don't say anything about it. When he's jumping for your hands, cross your arms so they're out of his grasp. Just be quiet about it. Wait for him to be still, and then when he is, click and treat.

2. Repeat it nine times. End the training session.

3. Now the time has come to introduce the cue. Jump up and get the puppy excited about it. Say things like "Calm," "Settle," or "Easy"— or whatever you want, just be consistent. And use a polite voice. Click and treat when he slows down.

4. After ten good repetitions, you don't have to press any more. Continue to take care of another dozen occasions. Then treat every other, then every third time, and then randomly, as you wean off the treats.

Tips: When your dog wraps around his collar or squeals with it, do not take it. If you remove it while he's pawing it, you're going to show him that his action is going to try to get you to take off the leash. Just make sure that the collar fits correctly so that he can't get his jaw or paw inside. Remember to check it out regularly, as puppies grow fast. A collar that fits perfectly one day could be too tight the next.

When you get your puppy used to wearing a collar, it's time for the leash to be attached. These are the measures.

Goal: The puppy must learn to wear a leash attached to his collar (or harness).

What you're going to need: leash, collar, treats.

1. Have the treats ready. Put the collar on your puppy and add the leash to it. Give three treats to your dog.

2. Let your dog pull the rope to a secure place where it won't get tangled. Supervise him closely to ensure he's healthy. Offer your dog treats randomly as long as he doesn't chew on his leash.

3. Gently take the rope and keep it. Give your dog a couple of treats.

4. Continue walking and inspire your dog to come along with you. If he's putting the brakes on, don't say anything. Just wait for him. Only apply enough pressure to tighten the cord slightly; don't yank it. If he starts walking with you, give him a lot of attention and a couple of treats.

5. Repeat until your dog allows you to tether it quickly. Use gentle pressure only if necessary. Don't use the leash to yank your puppy to you.

Bite Inhibition

Puppies have little needle-like teeth, and they like to put their teeth in everything, including you! Your puppy doesn't want to harm you or pretend to be "alpha." Chewing on something is a really natural puppy activity. Many dogs get more fun out of it than others. For instance, if you have a retriever, you may have a really mouthy puppy. Retrievers are brought up to put stuff in their mouths. This characteristic has been accentuated by a number of years of selective breeding.

Puppies chew when they're discovering their world. It doesn't sound like a very successful evaluation method — putting an object in your mouth to find out what it is — but it's a puppy's approach. Puppies chew stuff, too, because they're teething at around four months of age. They lose their baby teeth while the adult teeth pass into their gums. It can be very painful, so they chew to ease the pain in their gums. Puppies chew because it's fun too. They like to chew things, and their teeth are made for the job. Puppies are also chewing in battle with other dogs. When two dogs are running and fighting, they nip each other very playfully.

Puppies can even chew when they're stressed out. For instance, dogs who suffer separation anxiety and or have a fear of thunder sometimes chew doors and windows in their panic to escape. It isn't hatefulness; it's tension.

Some of the main concerns of new dog owners is that their dogs want to chew on them. Those little needle-like teeth can be very painful. It's incredibly necessary to teach your puppy bite avoidance during his younger months. It's going to be difficult to instruct once he reaches puberty.

Goal: Your puppy is going to know bite resistance.

What you're going to need: toys.

1. When your puppy's teeth touch your body, give it a pitiful, whiny "owwwww" as if you were severely hurt. Don't sound harsh or frustrated, or your puppy could just bite harder, thinking you're playing back. Act very sad about that.

2. Withdraw all the attention from your puppy. Your dog doesn't want to hurt you; he wants to play with you. When you're faced with a sign that he's hurt you, your puppy is likely to stop mouthing you immediately. Instead, he might start kissing you. Praise him for the kisses at this stage.

3. Take a toy that he's meant to chew on and give it to him. Praise him for it! You're trying to show him that chewing on you is unpleasant and hurts you, but you love it when he chews on his toys.

4. Do this every time your puppy's teeth touch your body. You're going to have to do this often because dogs have very short memories.

5. Be consistent with that. When you start using other strategies, you're going to have less success, and you're only going to annoy your puppy.

Another thing you should do to inhibit your puppy's mouthy actions is to stop having a rough time with him. If you or your family or friends are playing with your dog, and you think it's funny when he gnaws at you, then you're teaching him bad habits. You can't allow that to happen in some cases and not in others— it's just too overwhelming for a young puppy. There are a lot of games that you can play with your puppy instead of rough play. So, if your puppy isn't acting very cute, then the rough housing might need to stop. It's up to you to correct the action.

You know, if your puppy mouths you, it can be irritating. Don't scream at him, poke him in the face, put your fingers down his throat, shake him, or use some other physical abuse - it is only going to make the situation worse. Note that your puppy's just trying to play with you. You need to show him that he's not allowed to play with his teeth.

When you fight back, a very noisy puppy may think you're caught up in the game and bite down harder. Or, if you scare him, he will no longer chew on you, but he's likely to start chewing on other people. You're not going to tell him that chewing on you is painful; rather, you're going to teach him that you, actually, are frightened. Now he's going to chomp on your kids or your grandmother.

Each time your puppy's teeth strike your skin, show you're pained "owwww," remove your focus, and instead offer him a toy that he's allowed to chew on and lavish praise on him for that behavior. With consistency and repetition, your puppy will start running to your toy first, not your skin!

Trade

Property guarding happens when a dog attempts to discourage a human or other animal from taking something that he or she perceives as his or her own. It may block access to the object, or it may be tense, growl, snarl, or even bite. One way to discourage puppies from holding objects is to encourage them to give up their toys when you ask.

Also if your dog doesn't display any signs of protection, this is a successful avoidance practice.

Goal: When you cue him, your puppy will give up an object.

What you're going to need: two things that your puppy is likely to take in his mouth.

1. Give one thing to your dog, such as a toy. Let him calm down and chew on it for a couple of minutes.

2. Offer the other thing to him. When he comes to take it, thank him and give it to him. Pick up the original piece.

3. Repeat steps 1 and steps 2 three times. End the training session.

Handling

You're supposed to be able to touch your puppy all over his body without him nipping you, and without him flinching terror. This is one of the most important things you can teach your puppy. He's going to love when you touch him. You'll have to deal with him all his life, whether it's to search for fleas, give medication to his paws, cut his nails, clean him, or treat an injury.

Goal: The puppy is going to enjoy handling.

What you're going to need: treats.

1. Gently brush the ear of your puppy. Give him a treat right away. Touch his other ear gently. Give him a treat, please.

2. Gently brush the your puppy's paw. Give him a treat right away. Repeat all the paws.

3. Gently open your puppy's mouth. Treat.

4. Gently brush your puppy's ears. Treat.

5. Repeat all of the steps five times. End the training session.

6. In future training sessions, as your puppy gets more familiar with handling, start softly massaging your puppy's head, paws, mouth, and tail. If your puppy is getting squirmy or scared at any moment, slow down. Give lots of treats. Work up to where you can stimulate your dog when you're praising him and giving him occasional treats.

Tips: Some puppies have some places where they just don't like being handled. Some dogs, for instance, just don't like getting their mouths opened. If your puppy is particularly angry at this exercise, get him tired by playing with him beforehand. Use high-value treats and slow down the handling. For instance, instead of touching him with your hand, just use one finger. A step at a time, please. The time you take to do this exercise is going to pay off your puppy's whole life.

Nail Clipping

When your dog is used to being handled all over, you will take it further by encouraging him to enjoy getting his nails clipped and his fur trimmed, if necessary. Next, learn how to cut your puppy's nails properly. When you don't know how to do this, you should ask your groomer or vet to teach you how to do it.

Goal: Your puppy is going to love nail clipping.

What you're going to need: nail clippers, treats. Get a styptic paste or cream on your hand for if you nick his nail's quick and it bleeds.

1. Show the clippers to your puppy and instantly treat him.

2. Repeat it nine times. End the training session.

3. Repeat Steps 1-2 for one week.

4. Show the clippers to your puppy and touch one nail— but don't cut it! Give a treat right away. Repeat for a few nails and then finish the session. Gradually work up to the point that your puppy is confident scratching all of his paws. Just go as hard as your puppy is happy with.

5. When your dog doesn't like scratching his paws, it's time to cut a nail. Cut one nail, give three treats to your puppy, and end the session.

6. Repeat step 2, don't add more than two nails a day before you can remove all of his nails. Don't rush the process; doing so might set you back to your exercise, which would be difficult to repair.

Tip: You can use the same technique to introduce your puppy to a brush, a comb, or a scissor if you have to cut the fur between his paws. Only calm down and make every aspect of the training a good experience for your puppy.

Happy Vet Visits

It's inconvenient for puppies to be afraid of the vet. To take care of your dog, the doctor and vet technicians may need to do things that are uncomfortable for him, such as inserting a thermometer or giving him a shot. Such behavior will cause a puppy to fear visiting the veterinarian. There are also animals who are ill, in distress, and on medication that your puppy can hear and smell. It could be really scary.

It doesn't have to be like that, though. You should encourage your puppy to enjoy visiting a vet because he's going to have to do it all his life.

Goal: The puppy is going to have fear-free veterinarian appointments.

What you're going to need: clicker, treats.

1. Take the dog to the veterinarian clinic for a visit when he has no appointment. Press and handle all signs of outgoing behavior. Every time he comes forward to investigate something out of curiosity, click and reward. Each time he's happy to have you pet him, click and treat him.

2. Clarify to the employees why you carry your dog to their office and ask them to give him some treats. Some veterinary staff will be delighted to take part in this training because they want your puppy to feel comfortable visiting them, but please be aware that they are busy.

3. Repeat, ideally at least twice a week, until the puppy is ready to go to the veterinary clinic.

Tip: Don't encourage your puppy to go up to other animals in the veterinary clinic when you visit. This isn't nice, and it's not prudent either, as they may be there because they're ill. When your puppy displays any signs of anxiety or shyness, move very cautiously. Use several high-value treats.

Having your puppy enjoy the veterinarian office will depend on how friendly and comfortable your puppy is, of course, and how often you will be able to make such successful training visits.

If you can only make one, particularly during the crucial socialization time of your puppy before about sixteen weeks, then your puppy could still be afraid of the veterinary office.

CONCLUSION

The dog is an integral member of the family, and you want to do all you can to ensure that all parties work well together. This implies assisting the dog to adjust to the family environment by showing them right and wrong. This can be done through one-on-one dog exercises. Yet you need to learn the fundamentals of dog training yourself before you can properly teach your puppy.

Such simple dog training tips will help you get started on your way to guiding the actions of your dog. We also focus on communication strategies, which will be the first things you concentrate on in dog training. Starting there, you will have even more success in teaching more complex commands. The training of your puppy will be a wonderful adventure.